Scapa Flow

From graveyard to
resurrection

The original account of the greatest
scuttling in naval history
by the commander of the interned
Imperial German Fleet,
Vice Admiral Ludwig von Reuter,
with introductory narrative and
concluding story of the boldest
salvage of our time.

Published in the United Kingdom by
Wordsmith Publications
Chiltern House,
120, Eskdale Avenue,
Chesham,
Buckinghamshire HP5 3BD.

*Original account by Vice Admiral Ludwig von Reuter
published 1921*

This book first published June 2005

Joint Copyright
© Simon Mills and Wordsmith Publications

ISBN 1-899493-04-2

British Library Cataloguing in Publication Data
A CIP catalogue record for this book is available from the
British Library.

While every care has been taken in compiling the
information contained in this book, neither the publisher
nor the author accept responsibility for errors or omissions.

© Illustrations.
All illustrations are reproduced with the kind permission
of the Orkney Library Photographic Archive and the
von Reuter family.

Translation of Ludwig von Reuter's book, *Scapa Flow -Das
Grab der deutschen Flotte,* based on the 1940 translation by
I M N Mudie with consideration to correction of historical
errors, translation and current English.

Designed and typeset by
Communications Management International.

Printed in Great Britain by Bath Press

Cover design
Ian Garner

CONTENTS

Foreword to the original book by Ludwig von Reuter   4

Foreword   5

Setting The Scene   9
A narrative of the events which led to the greatest scuttling in history
Simon Mills

Scapa Flow
The grave of the German fleet
Vice Admiral Ludwig von Reuter

Chapter I   26
From the conclusion of the Armistice to the anchoring in the Firth of Forth

Chapter II   39
Interned in Scapa Flow – first reduction of crews – considerations of the position – my journey home

Chapter III   50
Again at Scapa Flow – protest of the government against the internment – the radical crews and the authority of the officers – The Red Guard and discipline – purging of the Soldiers' Council

Chapter IV   61
Change of flagship – second reduction of crews

Chapter V   63
The "scuttling" idea

Chapter VI   65
Influence of the internment on the ships' companies

Chapter VII   68
Preparations for the scuttling – last reduction of the crews

Chapter VIII   79
The Scuttling

Chapter IX   83
Justification of the scuttling – In prisoner-of-war camps at Nigg, Oswestry and Donnington Hall – return home

Von Reuter's Legacy   100
Reclaiming the Imperial navy
Simon Mills

Notes on von Reuter's text   110

Appendices to von Reuter's account   116

Bibliography   126

Index   127

FOREWORD

to **Scapa Flow** - *Grave of the German Fleet*
first published in 1921

There has been a long expressed wish for an account of the last few months of the existence of the German High Seas Fleet. In the following work I try to fulfil this wish and endeavour to give full details to justify the scuttling.

The political state of the country obliged me to keep back and suppress details of the current situation at the time and I have kept myself from embellishing the story. In planning this book I have put the little-known part first with the events from the signing of the Armistice to the scuttling being treated as one inclusive period. The second part - the justification of the sinking - is confined principally to the information and records I collected with this object.

The true story and motives of the German and enemy governments in their treatment of the interned fleet are not clear to me to this day. Accordingly I have until now had to build up my conclusions on bare facts which perhaps may not appear to be very pertinent to the uninitiated.

Apart from the scuttling itself, the period of internment has nothing dramatic, nothing outstanding about it. There were of course daily disputes, which, however, were only on that account important as they were over the struggle to keep the fleet for the country, and when that had become hopeless, they again cast their shadows over the last step towards the preservation of the welfare of the State.

Particular thanks are due to the printers and to Vizeadmiral von Ammon and to Fregattenkapitän Brehmer for their expert advice regarding the printing of the book, as well as to Kapitän-zur-See Oldekop and Marine-Kriegsgerichtsrat Loesch for the materials and diary so readily supplied.

Ludwig von Reuter
Vice-Admiral (Retired)

Gauernitz, Spring 1921.

FOREWORD
by the author of **The Grand Scuttle**
the Sinking of the German Fleet at Scapa Flow in 1919

THE LONG OVERDUE REISSUE of this memoir by Admiral Ludwig von Reuter of the Imperial German Navy in a new translation is both welcome and historically important. The word "unique" is overused but cannot be avoided here: Von Reuter is the only admiral who ever sank his own fleet. The scuttling of the Kaiser's High Seas Fleet as it rotted in internment seven months after the Armistice that ended the First World War is the greatest military act of material self-destruction in all history. In this book the man who secretly planned and ordered it explains his extraordinary action.

The author, stiff and "correct" in the strictest Prussian tradition, is no wordsmith, but despite any stylistic weaknesses it is a gripping account by the central figure in a remarkable moment of history: a resounding postscript to the terrible conflict that preceded it.

The German battlefleet that went to war in 1914 was a forced growth by which Kaiser Wilhelm II challenged the maritime supremacy on which the British Empire he so envied depended for its very existence. Technically and ship for ship the Germans outclassed the British. The fleet was founded on the "risk theory" of its main advocate, Admiral Tirpitz, who reasoned that a force big enough to take on the British Grand Fleet would cripple British power even in defeat. It would surely destroy more than enough of the King's ships to render the residue incapable of maintaining worldwide supremacy. Tirpitz recognised that the Imperial Navy would have to pass through a "danger zone" until its battlefleet acquired critical mass and could deter the British. The solution however was hearteningly simple − if also highly expensive - for a country which was then the world's leading shipbuilding nation: outbuild the Germans.

Nonetheless, the Kaiser's mighty battlefleet was one of the main causes of the First World War. Yet it fought only one major battle − at Jutland in 1916, which was a tactical victory but a strategic defeat for the Germans − and spent the rest of the war in or near port. It was the cheap little U-boats, initially discounted by both sides, that came closest to bringing Britain to its knees.

As defeat loomed for the German army on the Western Front, morale swiftly collapsed in the Imperial Navy. Unlike the British, German sailors on the big ships had the same relationship with their vessels as soldiers have with their tanks. The sailors lived in barracks and boarded their ships only to sail into the North Sea on exercise or to look for British targets, whereas British sailors lived aboard for long periods. So life for the skeleton crews in Scapa Flow, on ships never meant to be lived in, was gruelling and depressing.

The great German naval mutiny of 1918 had begun in the barracks and discipline collapsed, to such an extent that the naval command had the greatest difficulty in assembling the battlefleet, whose internment was demanded by the

Allies as an Armistice condition. But the ships remained German property and thus retained their reluctant German crews.

When I wrote *The Grand Scuttle* I was a correspondent for *The Times*. The most piquant irony for me in von Reuter's story was therefore the fact that the admiral relied for news on the censored, four-day-old copies of the paper supplied by the British guard-ships in Scapa Flow. On the eve of the scuttle he read that the Berlin government was refusing to sign the Treaty of Versailles. That meant renewed war and a British attempt to seize the ships (for which a detailed plan indeed existed). But in that four-day gap the government fell, unbeknown to von Reuter, and was replaced by men prepared to sign.

The ships were therefore sunk on a false premise. But the prime minister of the day, David Lloyd George, and other western leaders privately conceded that von Reuter had done them a favour – by forestalling quarrels over the division of the naval spoils.

One of the most moving sentences in von Reuter's official report describes their condition in internment. In a rare, poetic-romantic passage he sees them as *wehrlos, ehrlos* – disarmed, dishonoured. In the end neither they, nor especially he, were defenceless or dishonourable. It was on the deck of his flagship HMS *Revenge* that the commanding British admiral formally castigated von Reuter for ordering the mass scuttle – yet as every schoolboy used to know, Sir Richard Grenville scuttled the original *Revenge* rather than let her fall into enemy hands – the final irony in von Reuter's story.

Dan van der Vat, *April 2005*

Setting
The Scene

Admiral Ludwig von Reuter
(1869–1943)

The European map in 1914
showing the major naval bases of the Entente and the Triple Alliance

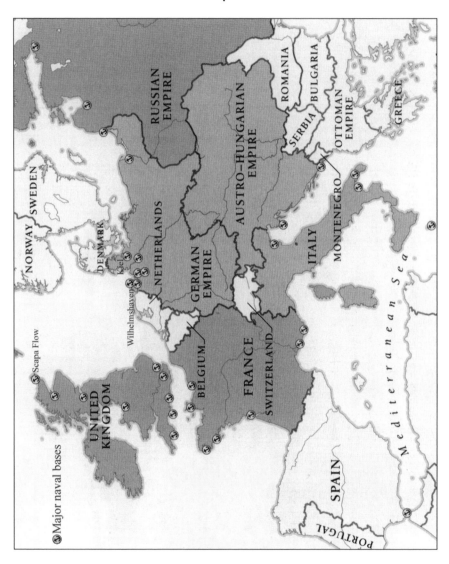

In 1869, Germany consisted of a loose confederation of numerous independent states that were largely influenced either by Prussia or Austria. Prussia had no naval aspirations at that time. It was, and always had been, a substantial land power, which, for reasons of its geographical location in Europe, placed far more emphasis on the army than its navy, so it may seem strange that Ludwig von Reuter, against this military tradition, would choose a naval career and one day command one of the largest and most modern battle fleets of its age. It seems all the more remarkable when one considers that the Prussian Admiralty was not created until 1853, when Prince Adalbert, brother of the Prussian king, Frederick William IV, was granted the title of Admiral of the Prussian Coasts. There was clearly a great deal of work to be done as the king was not inclined to make him Fleet Admiral for the perfectly justifiable reason that Prussia did not actually have a fleet.

Prussian shipbuilding capacity at this time was less than impressive, and the fact that most vessels in its coastal navy were built by foreign shipyards indicates their lack of dedication. The *Prinz Adalbert* and the *Friedrich Carl* had both been built in France, the *Prinz Adalbert* having begun life as the Confederation's *Cheops*, while the larger ships *Arminius*, *Kronprinz* and *König Wilhelm* were built in Great Britain, so from this it is clear that Prussian naval aspirations were not a priority.

If Adalbert was unable to find adequate numbers of officers from the merchant marine or the Prussian army he would use trained men from the navies of England, Denmark and Sweden. Nevertheless, realising the need for future Prussian officers he established a training school aboard the corvette *Amazone*. It was indeed therefore a misfortune when *Amazone* sank in a storm in November 1861, taking the entire 114-man crew with her. This setback seemed to have a profound effect on recruitment when the following year only three cadets applied. By 1870, however, Adalbert had a fleet of four ironclads based at Wilhelmshaven, although they proved to be a less than significant deterrent. The failure of the squadron to justify itself against the French fleet during the Franco-Prussian War, preferring instead to remain in port, resulted in the loss of forty Prussian merchant vessels.

It was against this background that Ludwig von Reuter was born at Guben, on the river Oder on 9th February 1869. He was the third son (and fifth child) of Eduard von Reuter, a colonel in the Prussian Army, although he would never know his father. Within a year of his birth France and Prussia would be at war and during the conflict Colonel von Reuter would die from wounds sustained at Spichern Heights, Lorraine in 1870, following which Bismarck's pursuit of the unification of the German Nation, and Prussia's emergence as the ultimate victor would lead to the creation of the German Empire in 1871.

For Helene von Reuter, life without her husband meant that the family had to move back to the town of Coburg, in what is now northern Bavaria. It was here that Ludwig would grow up, leaving school at the age of sixteen to join the navy as a cadet in 1885.

This marked a significant change of direction for a male member of the von Reuter family. His two elder brothers, Ernst and Alexander, had both chosen military careers in the German army, and in due course both would rise to the rank of general. In 1885 the German navy still lay in the shadow of the army; indeed, its lack of success against the French navy during the Franco-Prussian War had largely earned it the contempt of the land forces, and after Prince Adalbert's retirement in 1872 the navy had been commanded by a succession of army generals. As a result those vessels commissioned were designed more for coastal defence, with the generals considering the navy as little more than an extension of the army for the land battles that would follow against France or Russia, rather than as a tool for extending their power across the sea. Despite the fact that the French navy had complete mastery of the German North Sea coast during the Franco-Prussian War, Prussia had soundly beaten them on land, so perhaps it was not surprising that few in Germany saw any great value in a land power investing too heavily in any maritime ambitions.

It was only when Kaiser Wilhelm II ascended the throne in 1888, three years after Ludwig had entered the navy, that views began to change. Wilhelm's ideas about sea power were rather different from those of his generals, and he very quickly appointed a naval officer, Alexander von Monts to head the navy. Within six months there were plans for the construction of four 10,000-ton battleships, but after what seemed to be a promising start, confusion and lack of co-ordination between the German Oberkommando (High Command) and Reichsmarineamt (Imperial Naval Office) meant that the following ten years saw little progress in German naval capability. As a result the chances for promotion remained slow.

For young Ludwig it would be no different. After a year as a cadet he was promoted to midshipman and by 1888 he had attained the rank of Leutnant-zur-See, equivalent to a British Sub-Lieutenant, and it would be another six years before he would rise to the rank of Oberleutnant-zur-See (Lieutenant).

And then, on 6th June 1897 Rear Admiral Alfred Tirpitz was appointed State Secretary of the Navy, and with his arrival came a monumental change in outlook. In less than two-weeks he had drafted a memorandum for the construction of a German fleet, consisting of nineteen battleships, that could be ready within eight years. This was music to the ears of the ship-loving Wilhelm, who approved the document without hesitation. The following months were fraught with re-drafting and political manoeuvring, but on 26th March 1898 the Fleet Law was passed in the Reichstag. Tirpitz was effectively starting from scratch, and when the second Fleet Law was passed in 1900, doubling the number of warships in the 1898 Act, Tirpitz and the Kaiser had taken the first steps on a path of naval expansion that would set them on a collision course with Great Britain, turning the two countries from allies to potential rivals.

For Ludwig von Reuter, the opportunities for promotion were now in the ascendant. In 1898 he was promoted to Kapitänleutnant (Lieutenant-Commander), and at this time he found himself with the task of training the new cadets. One cadet in particular caught his eye and von Reuter became convinced that the young Erich Raeder would go on to carve out an illustrious career for himself. His instincts proved to be correct, as Raeder not only found himself serving as an admiral's staff officer at the Battle of Jutland, but would go on to become Grand Admiral and Chief of the Navy during the Second World War. For von Reuter, years later, this came as no great surprise.

The moment finally came when von Reuter would accept his first command, and in 1901 he was appointed to the armed yacht *Loreley*, which was stationed in the Aegean. At 920 tons and armed with only two 2-inch guns (one on the bow and one on the stern), *Loreley* was hardly an intimidating vessel. The Glasgow-built yacht was powered by one 700 IHP engine that enabled her to maintain eleven knots, and although she was considered a good sea boat, at times her tendency to pitch in a head sea could be serious enough to endanger the bowsprit. Even when the sea was beam on it resulted in quite a severe roll, but downwind it was a different matter and the extra sails made a useful addition to the ship's overall performance. The vessel always steered well although, curiously, she seemed to respond more easily when turning to starboard than to port.

While the *Loreley* may not have been a particularly prestigious command, the role she played was a significant one and von Reuter's principal duty during this time was to help maintain good German relations with the Sultan of Turkey and the King of Greece. In spite of an idyllic posting in the cobalt blue waters of the tranquil Aegean, this tour of duty was not without its hazards, and one particular incident was to result in considerable diplomatic friction.

One night the *Loreley* was secured for repair in the shipyard at the Piraeus. The crew had all been placed in barracks ashore and a solitary guardsman was standing watch over the ship. When the crew returned to the boat one morning they found that the guard had been murdered and the ship's iron safe, containing secret papers, stolen. Had the contents of the safe become known, the potential consequences could have had serious implications for von Reuter's future career, but he was not one to panic. Reasoning that that the iron safe was too heavy to have been carried far, he concluded that, as nothing unusual had been reported in the dockyard itself, the thieves might well have secreted the safe in the immediate vicinity hoping to return later to retrieve their booty in relative safety. Ordering his men to systematically search the harbour area, on land and water, his surmise was proved correct when the crew of one the boats felt a bump when its keel struck the submerged safe, as the craft moved across the surface of the water close to the *Loreley*,

Von Reuter's quick thinking had undoubtedly saved the day and possibly his career. There was little doubt that the robbery was politically motivated and this, combined with the murder of the sentry, necessitated its reporting to Germany where questions were even raised in the Reichstag. Clearly the affair had no lasting effect on von Reuter's record as he was promoted to Korvettenkapitän (Commander) in 1904, and four years later was serving as a

Fregattenkapitän in the Imperial Navy Office in Berlin. In 1910 he was appointed Kapitän-zur-See (captain) and in October of that year he took command of his first capital ship, the SMS *Yorck*.

Yorck was a Roon-class armoured cruiser of 9,533 tons with a main armament of four eight-inch guns. Her three screws gave the ship a maximum speed of 21 knots but in truth the 1901 design offered poor protection. Moreover, within one year of her entering service Britain had launched the all big-gun ship in the form of the battleship HMS *Dreadnought* which had powerful implications for not only the German navy but practically every naval vessel in the world. Von Reuter would remain with the *Yorck* until September 1912, when he was transferred to an administrative role at the Wilhelmshaven naval dockyard. This transfer to shore-based duties brought an additional attraction, as that same year he married his second wife, Johanna Brockelmann (his first marriage having been childless and ended by mutual agreement), and the couple would in time go on to have three sons.

This domestic bliss was, however, not to last very long. In August 1914 Germany found herself at war with Great Britain, France and Russia, and the High Seas Fleet, in itself one of the principal causes of antagonism with the British, would now have to justify its existence.

In October 1914 von Reuter's opportunity to serve his country was confirmed when he was given command of the modern battlecruiser *Derfflinger*, which was almost certainly one of the finest vessels of its type in the world at the time. *Derfflinger* was a massive ship, displacing over 26,000 tons and armed with eight 12-inch guns, her turbines could generate up to 63,000 shaft horsepower, giving her a maximum speed of 26.5 knots. With this nimble speed and armour plating, *Derfflinger* was a match for even the Royal Navy's modern Queen Elizabeth-class battleships, and although the British battleships carried heavier guns, the *Derfflinger* was without doubt one of the more prestigious commands of the High Seas Fleet.

Fearing an immediate head-on clash with the numerically superior British Grand Fleet, the High Seas Fleet preferred to mount hit-and-run attacks into the North Sea from German naval ports until they were in a position to face the British on more equitable terms. The speed of the German battlecruisers made them ideal for this task, and on 16th December 1914 *Derfflinger* took part in a daring raid to bombard the Yorkshire coastal town of Scarborough. Strategically the town was of no significance whatsoever, and it had been the German fleet's intention to draw the British Grand Fleet down from where it was maintaining a distant blockade of German ports out of its secure naval base at Scapa Flow. The strategy failed simply because the British fleet was unable to move south in time to intercept the German raiders, demonstrating that the British had conceded absolute control of the North Sea in favour of its overall strategic plan to maintain the blockade.

The next German expedition was not so successful. On 24th January Rear-Admiral Franz von Hipper led the three battlecruisers *Seydlitz*, *Moltke* and

Derfflinger, along with the heavy cruiser *Blücher*, into the North Sea to eliminate spy ships and lay mines in the Firth of Forth. Unfortunately for von Hipper, the British code breakers in Room 40 of the Admiralty had got wind of the plan and Admiral Beatty, along with the battlecruisers *Lion, Tiger, Princess Royal, New Zealand* and *Indomitable*, were waiting for them. It should have been a clear-cut British victory, but Beatty missed his opportunity. Gradually the British ships began to close on the German formation as von Hipper made a run for home, but rather than sustain the attack against the entire German line, the British battlecruisers instead concentrated their fire on the rearmost ship, the *Blücher*. Before long *Blücher* was devastated and finally capsized, sinking shortly after midday, taking 792 of her crew with her. In concentrating on the destruction of one isolated ship the British had allowed the three German battlecruisers to make good their escape. It could be said that Dogger Bank was not a particularly decisive battle for either the British or Germans. Although the loss of the *Blücher* effectively handed the day to the British, the Germans had escaped. The *Seydlitz* had also been heavily damaged and important lessons had been learned. For von Reuter, at least, the battle did have one satisfactory aspect, when immediately afterwards he was awarded the order of the Iron Cross (First Class).

On 3rd September 1915, von Reuter left *Derfflinger* to become commodore of the 4th Aufklärungsgruppe (Scouting Group). His flagship was the nine-year-old cruiser SMS *Stettin*, a Königsberg-class light cruiser of 3,800 tons mounting ten 4.1-inch guns, and it was in this role that he would take part in the greatest maritime gunnery duel that has ever taken place.

Even today the Battle of Jutland, known in Germany as the Battle of the Skaggerak, remains the largest clash involving naval gunnery of all time. Von Reuter's old command, *Derfflinger*, would play a prominent role and her gunfire was ultimately responsible for seriously damaging the battlecruiser HMS *Princess Royal*, but the *Stettin*, along with the light cruisers *Berlin, München, Frauenlob* and *Stuttgart*, were not designed to have a direct engagement with a dreadnought. Their task was to make initial contact with the enemy fleet and direct the heavier ships to their targets, while at the same time screening their own fleet from attack by destroyers or torpedo boats once action had begun. Considering the large number of smaller vessels turning at speed to evade incoming shells, together with constant manoeuvring to avoid collisions as well as attempting to remain out of the paths of the oncoming dreadnoughts, it is surprising that more ships were not lost. It was a role that ideally required quick-thinking officers with an ability to operate independently. At times it demanded considerable concentration of the flotilla chiefs and captains to maintain a reckoning of their own ships, let alone those of the enemy.

Von Reuter's flotilla was not directly involved in the heavier fighting, and it was only after nightfall, by which time the two fleets had lost contact with each other, that a confused game of hide and seek brought about a series of scattered night actions as the opposing scouting forces stumbled into each other.

Throughout the night there were nine skirmishes of this sort, and von Reuter would find himself heavily engaged in the third such encounter, when, at 22.35 hrs, *Stettin*, *München* and *Rostock* exchanged fire with HMS *Southampton* of the 2nd Light Cruiser Squadron. *Southampton* came off the worst in the gunnery duel, but she still succeeded in putting two six-inch shells into *Stettin*, which put her No. 4 port gun out of action and damaged a steam pipe to the whistle. Von Reuter would doubtless have continued the duel but escaping steam from the broken pipe obscured visibility, and a starboard turn for a torpedo shot was abandoned. *Southampton*, although badly damaged and on fire, still managed to launch a torpedo, which hit one of von Reuter's cruisers, the *Frauenlob*, in her port auxiliary engine room. She quickly went down with 324 of her crew; only nine men were rescued. *Stettin*, on the other hand, had suffered eight dead and twenty-eight wounded, but her ordeal was not quite over. The final clash between the lighter units of the two fleets had occurred just after 03.30. At 04.13 the pre-dreadnoughts *Hannover* and *Hessen* opened fire with their eleven-inch guns on what they thought to be a submarine. As it happens there were no British submarines in the area at all, but the *Stettin* was, and von Reuter came uncomfortably close to being sunk by friendly fire.

By dawn on 1st June all contact between the two fleets had been lost. The German ships limped back to their home ports, satisfied that they had done enough to win a great victory, although the final outcome of Jutland was, with the benefit of hindsight, not quite as they claimed. The High Seas Fleet had sunk more ships and inflicted a greater number of casualties on the Grand Fleet than they had sustained themselves, but in so doing the surviving German ships had suffered very heavy damage, and while the Grand Fleet remained fit and ready for action, it would be several months before the same could be said of the High Seas Fleet. More to the point, the Battle of Jutland had proved once and for all that the German navy would be unlikely to win a decisive surface action, and from that point on construction of battleships was scaled back dramatically as more emphasis was put into enlarging the U-boat flotillas. In the meantime, the capital ships of the High Seas Fleet remained in port and at anchor.

Von Reuter's duties with the 4th Scouting Group ended on 11th September 1916, when he was given command of the 2nd Scouting Group. On 25th November he was promoted to Konteradmiral (Rear-Admiral). His new flagship was the 5,440-ton light cruiser SMS *Königsberg*, which mounted eight 5.9-inch guns, and he would remain in that position for the next two years. While the battleships of the High Seas Fleet remained floating at their moorings, the cruisers of the 2nd Scouting Group were kept busy, and it was while leading a mine sweeping operation in the North Sea on 17th November 1917 that von Reuter's flotilla of four cruisers and ten destroyers were attacked by an overwhelmingly superior British force that included battleships and battlecruisers. It was a fight that von Reuter had no hope of winning, but his rear guard action as he fell back towards the larger supporting ships of the fleet resulted in the loss of only one trawler. Had the British not broken off the pursuit they may even have run foul of the German minefield towards which von Reuter was leading them. The 2nd Scouting Group did not escape totally unscathed, however. During the action, *Königsberg* took a direct hit from a fifteen-inch shell that fortunately failed to explode and after they returned to port the officers of his ship had the shell made safe and presented it to their admiral. This trophy became a cherished family heirloom and for many years would remain in von Reuter's living room.

The final year of the war continued to see the capital ships of the High Seas Fleet swinging idly at their buoys. As a result Reuter was also able to periodically serve as second in command of the 1st Aufklärungsgruppe, and on 11th August the position was made permanent. At this time there were wholesale changes in the High Seas Fleet. Admiral Reinhardt Scheer was appointed Chief of the Admiralty Staff, or in British naval parlance, head of the Naval Supreme Command. His deputy, Vizeadmiral Franz von Hipper, took his place as commander of the High Seas Fleet and von Reuter assumed command of the position vacated by von Hipper. Von Reuter now had control of the battlecruisers that Admiral von Hipper had commanded at Jutland. It was one of the most prestigious fighting commands in the fleet, but as the war reached its climax it was destined to be his last wartime command. By the autumn of that year the German army was in headlong retreat, and for the Kaiser and Germany the writing was on the wall, but neither officers or men could have anticipated what was in the mind of their supreme commander.

In October 1918, after months of inactivity, Scheer decided that one last throw of the dice could transform the German military situation. Few doubted that peace was just around the corner, but with the German army on the back foot and withdrawing to its own frontier, he believed, not unreasonably, that if he could inflict enough damage in one final confrontation with the Grand Fleet, it might considerably strengthen the German bargaining position at the peace negotiations.

On the evening of 29th October the battleships of the High Seas Fleet began to assemble in the Schillig Roads, just as they had done before Jutland, but almost immediately the plan began to unravel. On paper Scheer's grand design might have made good sense, but unfortunately he no longer had the courageous support which distinguished itself at Jutland. Many of his best officers and men had requested or been transferred to more productive duties with the U-boat flotillas, while the inactivity of the remaining crews at Kiel and Wilhelmshaven combined to make it very apparent that a combination of inexperienced men and poorly maintained ships of the High Seas Fleet would have sustained inordinately high casualties. These facts were not lost on the mutinous elements among the sailors based at Kiel, who were determined not to embark upon a mission they believed would end only in disaster when it was obvious that the war was all but over. The first rumblings of discontent were picked up on the battleships *Thüringen* and *Ostfriesland* as they were leaving

Wilhelmshaven, but it spread like wildfire and before long the officers on board the *Markgraf, Regensburg, Derfflinger* and *Von der Tann* had lost control to the point where the battleship *König* was unable to leave Kiel before mutinous dockyard workers had swarmed on board and torn down the war flag. With growing realisation that the High Seas Fleet was on the verge of self-destruction, von Hipper knew that the planned operation was doomed to failure and before long the signal: "Wiederrufen" ("Orders cancelled") was being sent around the fleet.

This microcosm of discontent and despair was by now echoing across the country. With the civilian population starving from the effects of the Allied blockade, the army incapable of fighting on, the country torn apart by political unrest and the formation of the many Workers' and Soldiers' Councils, the widespread demand for immediate peace and reform was irresistible. Any prospect of a constitutional monarchy was dashed when, on 9th November 1918, Phillipp Scheidemann, head of the socialist faction, proclaimed the new German Republic. That same day the Kaiser fled to exile in neutral Holland and two days later the Armistice was signed at Compiègne.

The war was over! Germany had sewn the wind and now the Allies were determined that she should reap the whirlwind. Articles twenty to twenty-four of the Armistice conditions amounted to virtual humiliation for the High Seas Fleet. Articles twenty and twenty-one demanded the immediate cessation of hostilities at sea, a German guarantee that all neutral shipping would be granted free passage and all Allied naval prisoners-of-war to be immediately returned, while article twenty-two demanded the surrender of the entire German submarine fleet, complete with armaments and equipment. It was article twenty-three, however, that had most relevance to von Reuter and his fellow officers, which stated:

> "The German surface warships, which shall be designated by
> the Allies and the United States of America, shall forthwith be
> dismantled and thereafter interned in neutral ports, or, failing
> them, Allied ports, to be designated by the Allies and the United
> States of America. They shall remain there under the surveillance
> of the Allies and the United States of America, only care and
> maintenance parties to be left aboard."

It could well have been the question on every German naval officer's mind concerning who may be charged with the dubious responsibility of commanding the High Seas Fleet on its outward and, as it would turn out, final voyage into captivity. After the Allied demand that the disarmed fleet should be transferred to the Firth of Forth under the command of an admiral, Admiral von Hipper pondered the various options open to him, and on the evening of 17th November he requested von Reuter's presence on board the flagship *Friedrich der Grosse*.

Aware of just how sensitive the issue was, von Hipper felt compelled to ask rather than order von Reuter to take command of the fleet. Indeed, for an officer as steeped in Prussian military tradition as von Reuter, whose first duty

16

was to his country, the task was about as painful as it could be. But in that the initial command was only presumed to be for the short period necessary to take the fleet over to the Firth of Forth before having it interned in neutral ports, von Reuter decided that in view of the Allies' threat to seize Heligoland and the consequences of a close blockade of the North Sea German ports, his internal struggle over personal honour was such that no matter how painful the duty, if it was something that had to be done in order to serve his country, then so be it. Furthermore, through his assuming command order would be maintained among the men, and would deny the Allies any justification for seizing the fleet under the pretext of crew indiscipline. So it was at noon on the 18th November he officially assumed command of the squadron.

At this time there was no indication that the fleet's ultimate destination would be Scapa Flow and the hope, perhaps rather naïve in the circumstances, was that once the peace negotiations were concluded the fleet would be allowed to return home. Von Reuter's main concern at this moment was to have the fleet ready for sea, barely twenty-four hours after he had officially assumed command.

That in itself was a triumph of organisation, as the squadrons were scattered in harbours from Kiel to Wilhelmshaven, and the socialist Workers' and Sailors' Councils, which were by that time in virtual control of the ports, offered little or nothing in the way of co-operation when it came to dismantling the ships. Fortunately Admiral von Hipper had managed to come to an agreement with the Councils, whereby the ships' officers would remain responsible for the navigation and conduct of the ships and, in the anarchic conditions prevailing, the right of the men to refuse an officer was withdrawn. Through exceptional diligence the ships were ready to sail at the appointed time and at noon on 19th November the High Seas Fleet assembled in the Schillig Roads for one last time. Von Reuter himself had taken the *Friedrich der Grosse* as his flagship, although with it ridden from top to bottom by mutineers and dissention it was a decision that he would later come to bitterly regret.

Against all the odds the High Seas Fleet made its rendezvous as arranged with the British Grand Fleet, under the command of Admiral David Beatty, at 08.00 hrs on 21st November, forty miles east of May Island in the North Sea. The "sufficient force" with which von Reuter had expected to be met turned out to be an overwhelming demonstration of sea power that appealed to Beatty's highly developed sense of drama. In spite of the fact that the German ships had all been disarmed, the sea was filled with Allied warships of every description. As the capital ships of the Grand Fleet took station along either side of the German fleet the humiliation was total.

The fleets dropped anchor in the Firth of Forth later that morning and for the next two days the Allies carried out a systematic search of every German vessel to ensure that they had been properly disarmed. Further degradation was heaped upon the Germans when Admiral Beatty ordered that at sunset on 21st November the German Imperial ensign should be hauled down for good. It was an order that von Reuter seriously considered challenging, but having obtained the agreement of the Sailors' Council to obey the British regulations, he would have had difficulty in challenging them himself. For the time being he could content himself with the fact that he was still entitled to fly his rear-admiral's pennant; in itself a legal symbol of sovereignty. The restrictions against flying the ensign was a further humiliation, but the intention for the German fleet to also be interned in the British naval harbour at Scapa Flow instead of neutral ports as originally specified, added considerably to the the High Seas Fleet's discomforture. By 27th November the seventy German ships had all been transferred to Orkney with little hope of an early return home.

If ever there was an example of the loneliness of command, the position of admiral in command of the interned German fleet must surely have been it. With only his officers to support him, for the next seven months von Reuter could neither count on the British nor his near-mutinous crews who for the most part exhibited little respect for naval procedure, their officers or themselves. It was also clear to von Reuter from the almost total lack of information from Germany that he was completely on his own. What little information he did receive was through the British newspapers, and even that was four-days-old. One thing was for sure, with the fleet now interned in a British port, von Reuter believed, even though care and maintenance parties had been arranged, it was becoming increasingly important that a principal officer should remain in command of the squadron in order to preserve what little discipline there was, and hopefully, ultimately to lead the fleet back to Germany.

Von Reuter returned to Germany on 13th December and it would not be until 25th January that he once again returned to resume his command. During his time away events aboard the German ships at Scapa Flow proved beyond a doubt that the presence of a resilient naval command was essential. During his absence an outbreak of trouble aboard the *Friedrich der Grosse* had completely undermined the authority of Commodore Dominik, who had assumed command of the squadron in his absence. For two months after his return, von Reuter was in constant conflict with the councillors aboard the flagship, and as if to further demonstrate a complete lack of respect for his authority many of the men took to stamping above his quarters in the hope that the constant noise would deprive him of sleep. Through a wily combination of exploiting the differences between the extremists and the more moderate members of the crew, along with tacit armed support from the British admiral, the extremists eventually backed down and agreed to return home on the next available transport which came on 17th February. Meanwhile, two insubordinate councillors which von Reuter, gambling on the support of the Naval Office in Wilhelmshaven, had seen fit to dismiss from the Supreme Council, were also homeward bound by 24th March.

Having finally disposed of the worst of the disruptive elements, political passions on the flagship and throughout the fleet settled down considerably. At long last von Reuter felt that he could finally transfer to a more compliant flagship. The change took place on 25th March, when the admiral transferred his flag to the 5,440-ton light cruiser *Emden*. In spite of the more limited space, it was a change that von Reuter and his entire staff welcomed. The environment and atmosphere aboard provided a welcome change to the anarchy on the *Friedrich der Grosse*. More importantly, the change to a more compliant flagship would prove to be a major benefit in the days ahead.

As the spring of 1919 wore on, the deadlock at the Paris peace conference began to cast an ominous shadow over the crews on the interned ships, and the lack of any official news from Germany confirmed to von Reuter that he was truly isolated. What little he could glean from the four-day-old copies of *The Times*, seemed to indicate that not only was Germany prepared to surrender the fleet in its entirety, but that the Allied terms were becoming progressively severe. It was increasingly apparent to him that the long-cherished ambition of taking the fleet back to Germany was ebbing away, and now von Reuter found himself contemplating an action that had hitherto remained only a remote possibility at the back of his mind.

Von Reuter's dilemma was profound. On a personal note, the surrender of the fleet would have been a painful ordeal, but honour dictated that he would have been prepared to make this sacrifice if Germany were able to obtain concessions elsewhere. At least then, the loss of the fleet would have served a purpose. What von Reuter and his fellow officers could not entertain was the thought that the High Seas Fleet would be given up without conditions. Although he would not go against the wishes of his government he would be damned if he would be the one to do it, and as the termination of the Armistice approached he requested that a signal be sent home in order to arrange for someone else to be sent over from Germany to carry out the final act of humiliation.

Von Reuter also had to consider the possibility that the British might try to take the fleet without the authority of the German Government prior to the signature of the peace treaty. If Germany were to refuse to sign the dictated peace terms, there was every possibility that the ships of the High Seas Fleet could be used against Germany in a resumption of the war. This was something that he could not even contemplate. Contenting himself in the knowledge that the Kaiser's standing orders ensured that no German warship should ever fall into the hands of the enemy, von Reuter arranged for the repatriation of a further 2,700 men of questionable loyalty, and on 17th June distributed a secret written order to his captains to prepare for the immediate scuttling of their ships upon receipt of a pre-arranged order from the flagship.

It may be that in preparing for the worst von Reuter had already foreseen the surrender of ships. It could also explain why on 13th June, he submitted a request for medical repatriation to Germany, along with a doctor's certificate which described the admiral as suffering from:

> "…*severe digestive troubles which give rise to the*

> *surmise that an internal complaint is developing, pains*
> *in the bowels, almost entire sleeplessness, severe headaches*
> *and daily attacks of giddiness, nerves strongly affected."*

Noting von Reuter's "unhealthy appearance" along with his "nervous and highly strung manner" when onboard HMS *Revenge* after the scuttling, Vice-Admiral Sir Sydney Fremantle, commanding the British 1st Battle Squadron, would later suggest in his report of 24th June that von Reuter's physical complaint may well have had a detrimental effect on his judgement.

Stomach problems aside, von Reuter knew precisely what he was doing when he wrote yet another telegram to Germany early on the morning of 21st June, requesting that the government send over another official to oversee the surrender of the fleet. However, the vision that greeted him when he emerged on deck later that morning to be confronted by the vacant anchorage of the British guard squadron, must have astonished him. At such a critical time, with the Armistice, to his knowledge, due to expire in a matter of hours, his mind might have raced at the decision of the British to choose such a critical moment to leave harbour. What von Reuter did not know was that the Armistice had been extended by three days following the resignation of Chancellor Scheidemann. Admiral Fremantle later contended that von Reuter had been unofficially informed of this extension before he took his ships to sea in order to complete the delayed torpedo practices that had been approved by the Admiralty on 18th June, but which had then delayed by bad weather. Von Reuter was equally unswerving in his claim that he had received no such notification, and with such little information available to him it was impossible to make sense of the situation. Was it possible, he thought, that the British were trying to lull him into a false sense of security by heading out to sea, only to unite with other squadrons and return in force to seize the German fleet?

Von Reuter, wearing his full dress uniform for the occasion, had only moments to weigh up his options. Fully believing that the Armistice was only hours away from expiring he fell back on his customary practise of mulling over familiar quotes that seemed appropriate to his situation. In this case he chose the words from act one of Schiller's *Death of Wallenstein*, which seemed more than appropriate:

> *"The time is o'er of brooding and contrivance,*
> *For Jupiter, the lustrous, lordeth now,*
> *And the dark work, complete of preparation,*
> *He draws by force into the realm of light.*
> *Now must we hasten on to action, ere*
> *The scheme, and most auspicious positure*
> *Parts o'er my head, and takes once more its flight,*
> *For the heaven's journey still, and adjourn not."*

And then, shortly after 10.30 a.m. the prearranged signal in the written order of 17th June ("Paragraph 11, Confirm") authorising the immediate scuttling of the fleet, was hoisted on the *Emden*. It was the first decisive step on one of the most extraordinary days in naval history. Within the next seven hours over fifty warships and the larger part of a once powerful navy would be lost forever. By the time the first British destroyers had raced back from their aborted torpedo practice, ten capital ships had already gone to the bottom of Scapa Flow. With little or no chance of the smaller British guard ships realistically being able to tow a battleship of over 20,000 tons, it is not surprising that most of the effort was directed to attempting to beach the light cruisers and destroyers. As a result only one battleship, the *Baden*, was successfully dragged ashore, while no more than three light cruisers, *Emden, Frankfurt* and *Nürnberg* were beached. The British might have been congratulated for the fact that they saved eighteen of the smaller torpedo boats in shallow water before they could sink completely - but not by the German commander. Von Reuter's major regret, however, was that the *Emden* was one of the few ships to be saved. His flagship constantly had a British tender alongside and he had decided to delay giving the final order to his own crew in case the heightened activity on board gave the game away to the drifter's British crews. His greatest regret, however, was what he considered to be the overreaction of the armed British seamen on the guard ships, though it has to be said that in spite of the haphazard shooting by the crews of the British drifters, the German casualties, as detailed in both the British report and German statements amounted to only eight men killed and five wounded[†], which would seem to be at odds with German witnesses' accusations of unbridled brutality.

By the evening of 21st June 1919, however, that was the least of von Reuter's problems. His reception by Admiral Fremantle aboard HMS *Revenge* was understandably cool, and Fremantle's accusation of treachery cut deep. Von Reuter disputed the charge and was understandably astonished when he was told of the extension to the Armistice. Nevertheless, for the rest of his life he would contend that any British officer, placed in his position, would almost certainly have acted in a similar manner.

The arguments for von Reuter's culpability with his officers, and the scuttling as an act of war continued for a further seven months, during which he was confined in prisoner-of-war camps at Nigg, Oswestry and, finally, the main officers' detention centre at Donnington Hall. In spite of intensive efforts, the British were unable to find any evidence to suggest that von Reuter had been acting under orders from Germany. Moreover, neither the British nor German governments were ever able to bring enought evidence against him to proceed with a formal trial. Von Reuter never swerved from his claim that he was acting on his own initiative. This, nevertheless, did not save the Fatherland from being burdened with additional reparations to make good the loss, although the value of the materials confiscated following the scuttling would never come near to

[†] The figures quoted are those of Admiral Fremantle in his report of 24th June, and although they differ slightly from Reuter's own account, their similarity does suggest that written observations made by other German officers were grossly exaggerated.

replacing that of the vessels which had been lost.

Germany finally signed the reparations protocol in January 1920, and on 29th January Vice Admiral Ludwig von Reuter, having been promoted to that rank on 12th December, was taken to Hull, where the steamer S.S *Lisboa* was waiting to carry him, along with the last remaining German prisoners-of-war to a hero's welcome in Wilhelmshaven.

In spite of the dramatically reduced German navy, now renamed the Reichsmarine, von Reuter's naval career was still not quite over. In the following months he worked on the official report into the scuttling and alleged British abuse of prisoners, but on 26th June of that year, less than five months after his heroic return, he received a letter from the navy requesting that he hand in his resignation, stating that they could:

> *"…no longer employ the services of Your Excellency in*
> *the navy in a position appropriate to your rank."*

It was a bitter pill to swallow, but Defence Minister Geissler had not lost sight of von Reuter's own unique contribution, concluding:

> *"I should not like to allow this occasion to pass without*
> *expressing thanks to you for the outstanding services you*
> *rendered the Fatherland in the navy. History will record*
> *your name as that of a man who contrived to make*
> *many German hearts beat faster in the dark days of*
> *1919."*

In many ways von Reuter welcomed the decision. He disliked the new naval regime and was not happy to be a part of the new *Reichsmarine* when his way of life was firmly rooted in the traditions of the Empire. Bowing to the inevitable, von Reuter accepted his enforced retirement, along with his naval pension, and moved from Wilhelmshaven to Schloss Gauernitz, in Saxony. It was here that he would write his book *Scapa Flow: Das Grab der deutschen Flotte*, first published in 1921, and two years later the family would finally settle in Potsdam.

At the relatively young age of fifty-four, von Reuter's retirement with three young boys was not destined to be a quiet one. Yorck and Derfflinger were named after the two ships that he had commanded when they were born, while the third he named Wolfgang. Between them they kept him very active, particularly on family sailing excursions in his small dinghy on the beautiful lakes around Potsdam. His son Yorck would later recall his father who, contrary to the classic image of a German militaristic family, while ensuring that his boys were well educated and behaved, would also allow them as much leeway as possible. Always full of humour and ideas, von Reuter would talk easily with them about history, politics, school and sport, and he was constantly quoting passages and proverbs from great German writers such as Goethe and Schiller. In spite of the joys of watching his family grow up, von Reuter was not one to remain idle for long and when the three children had left home he became a council member for Potsdam.

1939 brought with it a double honour. The first came on 9th February when, he received a telegram from the exiled Kaiser in Holland, who, after congratulating him on reaching his seventieth birthday, went on to say:

"With your act at Scapa Flow you saved the honour of the Imperial Navy. You thereby earned the ineradicable thanks of myself, the navy and the entire German nation." and was signed, " Wilhelm."

The second honour came on 29th August 1939, when he was promoted Honorary Full Admiral on the 25th Anniversary of the Battle of Tannenberg, although quite how his personal thoughts were in this respect is less certain as, according to his grandson, von Reuter was by no means an enthusiastic supporter of the Third Reich.

Less than a week later Great Britain and France were once again at war with Germany and his youngest son, Wolfgang, was killed in Poland during the first weeks of the Second World War. Then in April 1940 his eldest son, Yorck was captured by the British at Narvik while serving in the German navy during Operation Weserübung, the German code name for the invasion of Denmark and Norway. In many ways it was a curious case of history repeating itself as Yorck's ship, the destroyer *Hermann Künne* (Z19), exhausted of ammunition and fuel, was also scuttled in order to avoid capture by the enemy.

The war would bring one further tragedy for the von Reuter family when their eldest son, Derfflinger, was killed while fighting the Russians near Königsberg in East Prussia during the final weeks of the war, though fortunately von Reuter would be spared that pain. He continued his work as a Potsdam councillor right up to the end of his life, and on 18th December 1943, at the age of seventy-four, he collapsed and died of a heart attack while on his way to a meeting at the town hall.

At his funeral one of his former cadets, and no less a personage than Grand Admiral Erich Raeder, would give a reverential speech honouring von Reuter's unique place in German naval history, while his coffin, draped in the war flag of the old High Seas Fleet, and not that of the Kriegsmarine, was later carried to the Potsdam-Bornstedt graveyard, near Sans Souci.

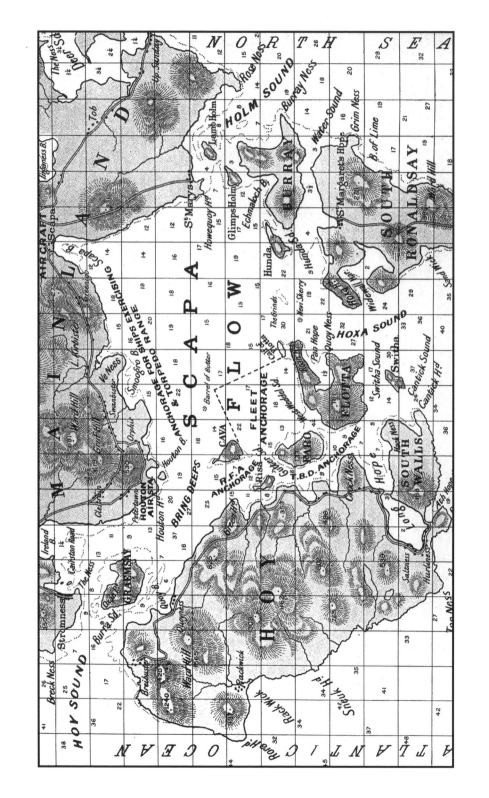

Scapa Flow
The Grave of the German Fleet

Vice Admiral Ludwig von Reuter

CHAPTER I

From the conclusion of the Armistice to the anchoring in the Firth of Forth

On the 10th November it became known in Wilhelmshaven that an Armistice with the powers of the Entente was being brought to a successful conclusion. Under a list of seven articles, ordering the disarmament of the German forces on land and water, appeared the particular one affecting the battleships, cruisers and torpedo boats of the High Seas Fleet, in which we are interested here. This was Article 23 of the Armistice terms. It runs:

> "The German surface warships, which shall be designated by the Allies and the United States of America, shall forthwith be dismantled and thereafter interned in neutral ports, or, failing them, Allied ports, to be designated by the Allies and the United States of America. They shall remain there under the surveillance of the Allies and the United States of America, only care and maintenance parties to be left aboard.

> The vessels designated by the Allies are:

> 6 Battlecruisers.

> 10 Battleships.

> 8 Light Cruisers (of which 2 are minelayers).

> 50 Destroyers of the most modern type.

> All vessels specified for internment shall be ready to leave German ports seven days after the signing of the Armistice. Directions for the voyage shall be given by wireless"

The Allies would respond to the non-fulfilment of the Armistice terms by the blockade of Helgoland. A few days later it was spread about Wilhelmshaven that the North Sea river estuaries were also threatened. Were this even just a rumour, sooner or later the Entente, to judge by their previous behaviour and what we expected, would stiffen their terms immeasurably. And the rumour did not fail to have an effect on the tranfer to the Firth of Forth of the High Seas Fleet.

Out of the conditional composition of the orders for internment the bad faith of the Entente was very clear. It was through this pressure, which the Entente could and did practise on the neutrals, that they could find no neutral ports for the German ships. They had, with the exception of Spain, whose harbours could not be brought into the question for our ships, never once thought it worth the trouble to worry over the preparation of a neutral harbour. They were certain that they would be able to get away with this omission concerning the German State. The request to the Spanish Government was also so worded that it was obvious that what was wanted was a refusal. The Entente has left the Armistice conditions unfulfilled and with premeditation, the imprisonment of the German ships at Scapa Flow.

To hasten the demanded dismantling, the ships of the High Seas Fleet were divided between the ports of the North Sea and Baltic corresponding to their home ports. The German naval command thought that the ships would leave these ports, either singly or in groups, for the voyage to the neutral ports imagined to be in Denmark, Sweden, Norway and Holland. For the dismantling and for the voyage to these ports it was essential that the ships' officers, who, with few exceptions, either because of a refusal of the ship's company or through the hoisting of the red flag had left their ships, should be reinstated on board. It was assumed that a certain limit of authority would be assured, so that ships' companies would no longer refuse to have officers and that the relationship between the government-appointed Soldiers' Councils and their officers would be regulated. The fleet commander succeeded in coming to an agreement with the 21st Committee of Delegates; the officers, under him alone, were responsible for the seamanlike conduct of the ships, in the internal affairs of the service the co-operation of the Soldiers' Councils had to be taken into account; in their own affairs the independence of the officers from the Soldiers' Councils was assured; the right of the men to refuse an officer was withdrawn. Even while these discussions were taking place the great majority of the officers returned to their ships, either through an overwhelming sense of duty or because they had been begged to return by their men.

The conditions of disorder on board and the many despicable actions of the Soldiers' Councils, and their incompetence to deal with the complicated organisation of ship's life, often left undone for days, had become intolerable to the crews. It need scarcely be said that the settlement of the fleet command was not recognised by all ships nor was it known how long it would last.

Due to the general unwillingness to work, the disarmament of the ships proceeded slowly, and that the removal of the disarmament gear was done with no care goes without saying. It says a lot for the excellence of our naval ammunition that no catastrophe arose out of its supremely careless handling.

During the disarmament came the news, though the order for the transfer of the German ships to the English harbours had not yet been included in the Entente's Armistice conditions, that in the taking of the ships over to England an examination of the agreed and stipulated disarmament would be held. How, and how far, the German Government opposed this new demand was not known; the protests addressed to the English command by the commander-in-chief were ignored. This new demand forced the ships to concentrate at Schillig Roads near Wilhelmshaven again. From here, commanded by the senior officer, they were to be conducted over to the Firth of Forth; a few days later came the demand from the English side that an admiral should take the ships over.

This order, to take the unbeaten German High Seas Fleet to the port of an enemy, set the corps of officers a new and peculiar problem. This was a performance of duty demanded of them, which lay outside all obligations of calling and position. This put before the officers a question of conscience, of extraordinary importance and difficulty! The solution to this question had to remain the affair of each individual officer. True, the superior officer can decide in his own mind on the solution and expect obedience from his officers, but still he cannot deny the right to the officer of differing in such a case.

The answer to the question was therefore dependent on each individual officer's understanding of 'honour'. Is the honour of an officer a thing in itself or is it intermeshed with the good of the State or subject to it? Both points of view must be given an equal value. For both, precedents can be found in the history of the Prussian officers corps. For the former can be cited the behaviour of von der Marwitz. When ordered by Frederick the Great to plunder the castle of Hubertusburg during the Seven Years' War[1], he repudiated the order as being against his honour and retired from the service. For the latter, the Treaty of Tauroggen, which Yorck concluded with the enemy, the Russians. The Prussian officers corps demanded of the king that Yorck should be brought before a court of honour; the king declined[2].

I decided personally, therefore, as the question of the appointment of an admiral for the leading over of the fleet to the Firth of Forth had become a burning one for me, that honour, in this case, was to serve for the good of the State. I considered that the blockade of Helgoland and the North Sea estuaries would be such a serious thing, that I personally could play no part in the harm this would do the German State if I could avoid it.

There was no question in my mind that through the blockade of the North Sea ports and Helgoland the Entente would seize the German fleet as well, and that by observing the state and temper they had been brought to by the revolution, this would take place without hindrance from the ships' companies of the High Seas Fleet.

Further, the Armistice only ordained that the High Seas Fleet would be taken over to an English port to prove their disarmament. From there they would be sent for internment in neutral ports.

That the ships to be taken over were to be brought to ruin was to be anticipated from the English character. Anticipation is, however, no certainty. The knowledge that we would be betrayed had first to be a matter of fact. The betrayal would give us back our freedom of action; we could then do what we liked with our ships, we could also sink them.

To sink the ships before the voyage to England was unhappily out of the question, because of the temper of the crews and by the total loss of authority of the officers. Time, however, could alter the situation appreciably and improve it.

Were the officers corps not to participate in the transfer of the ships to England and to leave their ships, then would the crews in their aversion to a fresh outbreak of war, themselves have taken the ships over to the enemy, or else would have handed them over in German ports? In both cases it seemed certain the Entente would not fail to profit by the least opportunity to take the ships into their own possession, and apparently legally. The revolutionary German crews had hounded the officers out of the ships. Their press would then, of course, have announced to the whole world that the English admiral, owing to the inattention of the German officers to their duty in having deserted their ships, was with regret compelled to seize the German ships, as on no account could these be left in the hands of a lot of murderous sailors. A great part of the German press had without question, made announcements in this vein. Fortunately the announcements of the newspapers had not influenced the sea officer. For him his instinct alone would guide him; what is done to the ships of the High Seas Fleet is done through the officer - he would participate as an issue of honour.

I had myself come to a clear conclusion the officer must take charge himself of the leading over of the fleet.

In this way a certain amount of discipline and order would be kept on board the German ships, and thus would deny the English the opportunity of seizing the ship under the pretext of the lack of discipline on board. Should the question of who should take the fleet over come my way, I would not refuse provided no suitable admiral for this unhappy task could be found. I did not come to this decision easily.

I will not say that at this time I had not already had the idea of taking a personal part in the sinking of the High Seas Fleet; I thought far more of returning to the Homeland before the beginning of the voyage from the Firth of Forth to the neutral ports. Plans at that time, therefore, could not of course be laid as to what to aim for next. However, soon after the voyage on to Scapa Flow, the suddenly overwhelming feeling grew in me that I should provide a way out of internment worthy of the High Seas Fleet. In the prosecution of my resolve, to take over the leadership of the fleet, I had to exact the compliance of the officers. Similar trains of thought seem to have exercised the mind of the late commander-in-chief, Admiral von Hipper, whilst he was himself preparing the High Seas Fleet for the voyage over to England. Later too I found many officers in the fleet whose convictions differed little, if at all, from mine. I must again emphasise here, that if it is said or written that the German fleet was surrendered and delivered over to the enemy by German sea officers, we officers knew what we were doing!

The Allies still had to give instructions for the implementation of the Armistice conditions regarding the sea forces. On the 12th November the English commander-in-chief therefore requested that the German commander-in-chief would send an admiral to the Firth of Forth for a conference. Konteradmiral Meurer[3] was appointed for this duty. He reached the Firth of Forth on board the light cruiser *Königsberg* on the 15th November. The conferences took place on board the English flagship *Queen Elizabeth* on this day and the next. Admiral Meurer communicated the results to Admiral von Hipper during the morning of the 18th November. These, in substance, comprised the following:

(a) Proceed to the Firth of Forth and anchor in the outer roads for confirmation of the ships' disarmament.

(b) Rendezvous 40 nautical miles due east of May Island on the 21st November at 8 a.m. G.M.T.

(c) To get there steer for position 'S' (a particular point on the track which led through the North Sea minefields) and the South Dogger Light Ship

(d) Course of approach 270° at 10 knots. Formation: ships in line ahead, battlecruisers in the van then battleships, light cruisers, with the destroyers in the rear.

(e) Guns to be secured for sea, trained fore and aft.

(f) A suitable (English) force will receive the German ships at the rendezvous and conduct them to the anchorage.

(g) In each case an English light cruiser, with a blue flag at the masthead, will place itself at the head of each group of German ships and lead them to the anchorage.

(h) Plan of the anchorage in the Firth of Forth.

(i) 1. Fuel required: For 1,500 nautical miles at 12 knots from Schillig Roads; in addition, sufficient for auxiliary machinery until the 17th December.
2. Provisions required: For 10 days for the steaming party and until the 17th December for the ship-keepers.

Incidentally, it appears that the English commander-in-chief, Admiral Beatty, was informed at this conference that the battleship *König* and the light cruiser *Dresden* would not be ready to sail at the appointed date, but would follow over as soon as possible. They joined the fleet at Scapa Flow on 6th December. The *Mackensen*, which had been selected as the sixth battlecruiser, was still building. The negotiations in regard to her took some time to come to a conclusion, but eventually, in January 1919, the battleship *Baden* was delivered at Scapa Flow in her place.

On the evening of 17th November the commander-in-chief, Admiral von Hipper, requested my presence on board the flagship. He disclosed the English demand that an admiral should lead over the German fighting forces to the Firth of Forth. Out of the admirals of the High Seas Fleet the name of Admiral Meurer and mine were in question for selection for this duty. As it was uncertain, in the prevailing foggy weather, whether the former would be back in sufficient time from the Firth of Forth, he requested me, in these circumstances, to take over the leadership of the squadron. It was only for the short time necessary to take the ships over to the Firth of Forth, and then after interning them in neutral ports I would return home again. I pointed out to him the grounds on which it made it hard for me to take over the squadron, but I placed myself at his disposal for this duty in the event of Admiral Meurer being unable to get back in time. I held that this officer was the more suitable as he had conducted the negotiations with the English commander-in-chief and therefore was best qualified to judge what the English requirements would be and whether these demands should be met or opposed. Admiral Meurer returned on the morning of 18th November and therefore with plenty of time to take over the leadership of the squadron. In spite of this the commander-in-chief, during the morning of the 18th November, requested me to take over the squadron, as Admiral Meurer had been chosen as a delegate for the Armistice Commission in Wilhelmshaven and could not be dispensed with or removed from this duty.

At noon on the 18th November I assumed command of the squadron. It lay scattered in various harbours. On 19th November, at twelve noon, the squadron was due to leave Schillig Roads for the voyage to England. An enormous amount of work had still to be got through in the few remaining hours.

From the commander-in-chief, Admiral von Hipper, I received the following written orders:

1. .... (Irrelevant)

2. The ports of internment selected, after the search of the ships
   in the Firth of Forth and after taking the English escort
   aboard, are not known. All steaming parties will remain
   aboard until their ships enter the ports of internment. Only
   ship-keepers will remain on board when the ships are in the
   ports of internment, the remaining portion of the steaming
   party will be sent back by transports. Admiral Beatty has
   assured me that the names of the ports of internment and
   the dates on which the transports must reach these ports will
   be communicated to me in plenty of time. Suitable reports
   and orders will then be issued.

3. After the taking over of the squadron by the English cruiser
   escort (40 nautical miles east of May Island) all wireless
   traffic is to cease, unless the leader of the escort, or, later, the
   commander-in-chief Grand Fleet, allows it by orders
   mutually agreed.

Signed: von Hipper.

Admiral Meurer explained to me verbally the written arrangements he had come to with the English commander-in-chief and gave me his personal impressions, which induced me to exercise the utmost care and reticence in my dealings with the English fleet commander. Admiral Meurer mentioned that in his opinion the English had not the slightest intention of allowing our ships to go to neutral ports; I learnt for the first time many months later that Admiral

Beatty did not appear to have reckoned on the German fleet reaching the Firth of Forth intact. This information, however, would have been of no use to us officers in our then state of helplessness and it would only have made the hard road to the Firth of Forth even harder.

The staff for the squadron was quickly collected. Fregattenkapitän Ivan Oldekop was won over for the duty of chief of staff. He was of the utmost service to the squadron; I had the utmost trust in him and his practical personal character made work with him easy and stimulating. The load of the work was never too heavy for him, and although he stood daily 'in the line of fire,' in disputes with the radical elements, his attitude and services never became disagreeable. He should take full credit for the successful results of the squadron. Let me here express my warmest thanks to him and to the gentlemen of my staff for their self-sacrificing co-operation in the little-extolled problems of the squadron. On this last journey of the High Seas Fleet they have again given of their best and by their personal conduct made my duty bearable. In particular, I must mention the leader of the torpedo boats, Korvettenkapitän Hermann Cordes - in him were united all the personal and service attributes in the highest degree, which a leader of torpedo craft should have. The fresh cheerfulness and depth of his character, his high understanding and aptitude which he displayed in his leadership and handling of officers and ships' companies, were of the utmost use to the squadron and will bring him honour for all time

The squadron had the name of *Uberfuhrungsverband* and was considered as a squadron detached from the High Seas Fleet. The battleship *Friedrich der Grosse* was chosen as flagship.

The assumption of command was made known to the squadron in the following words:

> 'I have today taken over the command of the squadron. I know
> that I am at one with the ships' companies, in that for the voyage
> over everyone will do his duty, so that the Fatherland will soon
> have peace.'

During the evening of the 18th November I embarked in the *Friedrich der Grosse* with my staff. She took us, still by night, to the Schillig Roads. A portion of the squadron was already assembled there, but it was hardly possible to name them owing to the prevailing disorder; further it was not known if they were disarmed according to the regulations, nor if they were provided with the requisite amount of fuel and provisions. It was impossible to interfere with this and it had to be left to lucky chance whether at the appointed time - at nine o'clock in the morning of the 19th November - all the ships and torpedo craft would be at the appointed place and ready for the journey over. On the morning of the 19th November it became apparent that the lucky chance had come to pass and that the squadron was assembled.

At a meeting I instructed the senior officer and the commanding officers of

Ludwig von Reuter (right) aged 6, with his brother Alexander. (Circa 1875)

Alexander and Ludwig in 1885. Alexander wears his army uniform, while Ludwig (right) is dressed in the uniform of a naval cadet.

Above: *Grand Admiral von Koster poses with the admirals and commanders of the battle fleet (circa 1907). Korvettenkapitän von Reuter (circled) stands at the rear.*

Right:
Commodore
Ludwig von
Reuter, shortly
after his
promotion in
1916.

Admiral Sir Sydney Fremantle, von Reuter's jailer at Scapa Flow and commander of the British 1st Battle Squadron in June 1919.

Vice Admiral Ludwig von Reuter. This photograph was taken in 1920 following his release from captivity. An unusual feature of von Reuter's uniform is the crown on the left sleeve; the symbol of the old Imperial Navy. Following the establishment of the German Republic, the crown had been replaced with a star.

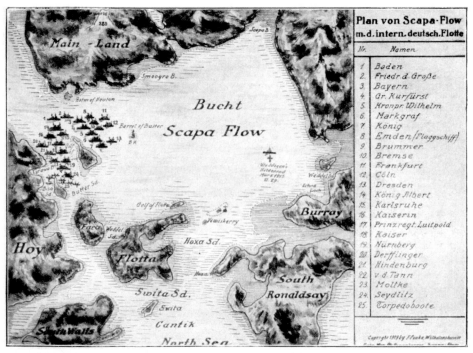

Plan von Scapa-Flow m.d. intern. deutsch. Flotte	
Nr.	Namen
1.	Baden
2.	Friedr. d. Große
3.	Bayern
4.	Gr. Kurfürst
5.	Kronpr. Wilhelm
6.	Markgraf
7.	König
8.	Emden (Flaggschiff)
9.	Brummer
10.	Bremse
11.	Frankfurt
12.	Cöln
13.	Dresden
14.	König Albert
15.	Karlsruhe
16.	Kaiserin
17.	Prinzregt. Luitpold
18.	Kaiser
19.	Nürnberg
20.	Derfflinger
21.	Hindenburg
22.	v. d. Tann
23.	Moltke
24.	Seydlitz
25.	Torpedoboote.

Above: A contemporary German plan of Scapa Flow showing the location of the individual ships.

Wilhelmshaven on 31st January 1920. Vizeadmiral Ludwig von Reuter, still wearing the military overcoat given to him by Rittmeister (cavalry captain) von Dresky, is reunited with his wife and two sons on the deck of the S.S. Lisboa.

Above: Von Reuter with sons Wolfgang (left) and Yorck (right). Wolfgang would be killed in Poland in September 1939, while Yorck would go on to be captured by the British at Narvik in April 1940 and spend the rest of the war imprisoned in Canada.

Ludwig von Reuter as a seventy-one year old Councillor in Potsdam in 1940.

Above: The funeral of Admiral Ludwig von Reuter on Thursday 23rd December 1943, at the Heiligengeistkirche in Potsdam. The coffin is draped in the war flag of the old Imperial Navy, rather than that of the Kriegsmarine. Von Reuter was not a strong sympathiser of Hitler's Third Reich, yet in the climate of the time the officers gave the Nazi salute. The church was subsequently destroyed by the Russians in 1945, but later rebuilt by the Americans.

Left: The headstone on the grave of Admiral Ludwig von Reuter, in the Bornstedt graveyard, Potsdam.

the ships briefly on the principles that were to guide the conduct of the squadron. I had taken over the squadron purely so that the bitterly necessary order and peace of the State could not again be in question. I put the same motives before the officers of the squadron. The many points agreed upon between the fleet and the 21st Committee of Delegates were then gone over, especially that the seamanlike handling of the ships remained in the hands of the executive officers, and that the Soldiers' Councils were excluded from this. One question, which had not been cleared up, was what colours were to be worn? No naval officers would have gone to sea under the red flag. It was arranged to hoist the war ensign; a red emblem was indeed hoisted at the foremast, but as the flagship began to move it was hauled down. Finally, orders were issued regarding the dress and conduct of the ships' companies during the journey to the Firth of Forth and about the official communications between the English naval authorities and ourselves. In this, owing to the disapproval of the English, the Soldiers' Councils were to have no part. The German officers were to reject permission were it proffered to them during the internment. They were to tell their ships' companies that I would shield any member of the squadron, as Germans, in relation to the English. However, the officers were ordered to be cautious towards the men and to abstain from propaganda; this would lead to no success and only give instigators the opportunity to agitate against the officers.

After this meeting a similar one of the Soldiers' Council took place to choose the squadron delegate, or Head Soldiers' Councillor as he called himself later. A head-man and two delegates were chosen. The first had never been on board a ship before. He must have been smuggled on board the flagship by the machinations of the local revolutionary authorities in Wilhelmshaven with a forged order from the Admiralty. To understand the ideas which the Soldiers' Councillors had of themselves, the words with which one of them greeted the chief of staff after election are typical: "Well, I have now taken over the command of the squadron, and you are my technical adviser." The chief of staff explained the consequences of hoisting the red flag to the Soldiers' Councillors; that it was a pirate's flag and would be fired on immediately, and the ship wearing it destroyed, anywhere on the high seas. This damped their enthusiasm to cross the North Sea under the red flag to such an extent that the Soldiers' Councillors turned repentantly back to the better protection of the old and tried war flag. They thought, however, that they could not give up a small red emblem at the foremasthead; the enthusiasm for this too died down and soon after leaving the Jade estuary it was hauled down.

Voyage to the Firth of Forth.

The time for the squadron to put to sea was fixed for 12 noon. It had to be postponed for two hours, as one of the large cruisers could not raise steam in time.

On a sunny, quiet, autumn day the long row of ships and torpedo boats got into formation, in the van the five battlecruisers *Seydlitz, Moltke, Hindenburg, Derfflinger,* and *Von der Tann,* then the Fourth and Third Squadrons, led by the *Friedrich der Grosse.* These were followed by the light cruisers and these again by the torpedo boats. They steamed out into the North Sea as they had so often done during the war, silently majestic, only, this time, not to fight for home and people.

We passed Helgoland[4], lit up by the rays of the sinking autumn sun - it glowed in all colours. Helgoland was worth this journey! That was a consolation to us officers. Then we passed over the battlefield of the 17th November 1917,[5] ever further towards England.

The course we were instructed to follow led us through mine-strewn waters. Shortly before, lightships were laid out for us so as to make navigation by night safe, and the course was arranged to keep us clear of mines. Nevertheless, torpedo boat *V30* struck a mine and sank. The casualties were two dead and three wounded; the crew was taken on board another torpedo boat. The English, nevertheless, demanded a substitute to replace this torpedo boat, lost purely by accident, which was supplied by the German Armistice Commission.

The 20th November was again a sunny day, only somewhat misty. The monotony of the day was broken by the sending of a dispatch boat with letters from the fleet command to the English commander, and during the evening by the news that the light cruiser *Cöln* had leaks in all her condensers, but would attempt to follow us. Another small cruiser was ordered to stand by the *Cöln* and if necessary to take her in tow.

And now, dawn of the 21st November, the day settled for our arrival at the Firth of Forth. This day too was sunny, but still very misty. Our hope that fog would hide us unfortunately did not come true. All the time the mist diminished the most impressive part of the picture for the enemy. Punctually at 8 o'clock the rendezvous was made with the English forces, which were to lead us through the obstructions. An English cruiser took station at the head of the line of heavy cruisers and battleships and with increased speed headed for the Firth of Forth. Ever more English ships, and ships of the Entente, appeared out of the foggy background, taking station ahead of us or shutting us in, on both sides. Even a French warship appeared, an unusual sight in the North Sea. Over us cruised airships and aeroplanes. All the English ships were cleared for action. The enemy could hardly believe that the victor of the Battle of Skagerrak[6], this most feared German fleet, really was disarmed, and, further, would not use this last opportunity to overwhelm the English fleet treacherously. Still, for such a design the very elements were lacking in the squadron, as they could not maintain a speed of more than 11 knots.

Again and again the wind brought us the noise of the English cheering. We had the feeling that a sense of shame should have drowned out this ecstatic shouting, to have the unconquered fleet delivered into their hands, which had shattered England's historic mastery of the sea at Skagerrak.

The English announcements reflected most unfavourably on the deportment

34

of our ships' companies and on the appearance of the ships. Only English presumption could expect that we would dress up our crews in their Sunday best and paint up our ships solely to do them honour. The ships kept their station as well as it was possible for the officers to achieve it, considering the unreliability of the boilers and engines; unfortunately a bunching of the line did take place, which caused one or two ships to sheer out. A short time before anchoring, the English ships filed past their fleet flagship and gave their Admiral Beatty three cheers. About 3 o'clock in the afternoon the squadron anchored in the anchorage allocated to them; the anchoring itself proceeded with no particular trouble.

About 4 o'clock in the afternoon a wireless signal arrived from the English commander-in-chief which read: "The German flag will be hauled down at 3.57 in the afternoon and is not to be re-hoisted without 'permission.' "

English politics favour the dramatic gesture. By this order England wished to announce her final victory over the German fleet to the world.

Considered in the light of international right, the hauling down of the flag could not be considered as deciding the issue of the sovereignty of the German ships. The sovereignty of the squadron remained as it was, as they kept their command flags, the admiral's flag and the captains' pendants. It is to be presumed that the principal part of this gesture, the hauling down of the command flags, must have been overlooked. In the later judicial examination, on the sinking of the German ships, initiated by the English Government, real surprise was expressed at this omission.

This view of the squadron with respect to international usage accepted until now, e.g. in the Russo-Japanese War, that it was not customary for interned ships to haul down their flags, was the cause of the lodging of both written and oral protests against this striking of the flag. We called on his feeling of chivalry as well, that between worthy foes such presumption was not customary. The protest was answered with a refusal based on the allegation that a state of war still existed between England and Germany. This decision was declined in a further letter to the English commander-in-chief. At the same time the German commander-in-chief was informed of the protest in the following wireless message; it is here given from memory as the letter of protest itself was lost in the sinking:

'The English fleet commander ordered the war flag to be hauled down at evening parade on the 21st November and that it was not to be re-hoisted without permission. I have protested against this; this is an internment. Neutral and enemy harbours according to the Armistice stipulations are the same. As the hauling down of colours in neutral ports would not follow, this should not be allowed to happen in enemy ports. The English fleet commander has answered with a refusal. Only hostilities have ceased, the state of war still exists. No enemy ship can be permitted to wear her flag in British ports as long as they are under supervision. I cannot accept this decision.'

On the very evening of our arrival the second in command of the Grand

Fleet, Admiral Madden, sent his chief of staff, Commodore Hodges, with some officers and interpreters, on board my flagship. He gave me the instructions for the German ships:

(a) For state of readiness of machinery, shackles of cable to lie at, boat traffic in the Firth of Forth, lights to be displayed at night, wireless traffic, censorship, signal communications with the English ships and the postal instructions.

(b) In order to confirm the ships' disarmament; on the 21st November a preliminary search was to take place, and on the 22nd November a thorough examination.

The English admiral undertook to arrange the delivery of these instructions to the individual ships. In the conversation with Commodore Hodges it emerged:

1. That there were no cases of infectious disease, such as influenza, in the squadron. Serious cases were to be sent to an English hospital ship as previously indicated by the English admiral.

2. That the light cruiser *Cöln* had not arrived, and that the extent of the damage to her machinery was not known at all in the squadron.

3. A verbal protest against the order to haul down the colours was lodged. Commodore Hodges himself made out that he knew nothing about this order of the English commander-in-chief

4. The letters of the German commander-in-chief were handed over. I impressed on the mind of the fleet commander the necessity for maintaining the number of men in the ship-keeping parties for particular ships.

5. In answer to my question as to which of the neutral ports we would be interned, came the reply that they were not known.

6. The English admiral informed me that should I wish to speak with him I should announce my wish to him. For the time being I had no reason for doing so

In the instructions regarding boat traffic it was laid down that boat communication from ship-to-ship was forbidden and that no boats were to be lowered. Fire would be opened on any boats lowered in contravention of these orders. This regulation was at once made known to the ships to avoid incidents. In spite of this a torpedo boat, which had not yet received the order and did not know about it, had blundered. After an investigation by the English admiral he informed me, late at night, that the matter had been cleared up and settled.

The 22nd November was given over to the examination of the ships. The

English Examination Commission consisted of a collection of naval officers, warrant officers, petty officers, and men, all together. They appeared to be drawn from English ships of similar classes to the ones of ours they were to search. The English ordered that the German ships' companies were to remain on deck, away from the guns, that all spaces and lockers were to be left open, that plans of the ships, states of the ships' companies, interpreters, and guides were to be kept ready.

The examination for confirmation of disarmament was carried out thoroughly. For instance, in the bunkers the coal was turned over, in the magazines the chests and boxes that happened to be stowed there were opened. The English appeared to have approached the duty of examination with the confirmed idea that the disarmament had not really been carried out; they could not give us the credit for carrying this out to the letter. They found nothing to which they could take exception; in fact, it appeared that the disarmament had been too thorough in that breechblocks, gunnery and torpedo control communication pipes had been removed. The English could not disguise a real surprise at the excellence of our materials. As an example of this I quote the opinion of an American naval officer as given to the captain of the *Bayern* after he had been over her a little later on: 'You could not possibly have realised what a weapon you held, in the shape of your fleet, against England. Had you known this and made use of it events would have turned out very differently. No English ship can compare with yours, in particular I refer to the *Bayern*.' Now, we knew what our ships were like. It was not the good fortune of the naval officers to see what they wished carried out, that was how things stood: we had to drag round the leaden weight of falsely-understood, foreign-led politics with us; in addition, after the Skagerrak the enemy had avoided a further battle with us, he fell back on the use of his favourable geographical position and spared his fleet.

The personal conduct of the individual representatives of the commission was very varied; it ran the whole scale from the utmost coldness to a lively sympathy for the position and condition of the German naval officers. The Soldiers' Councillors had posted themselves at the gangway wearing white armlets and red rosettes. The English officers and men regarded their forwardness with the utmost disfavour. This cold douche annoyed them but they learnt nothing from it. The attempted fraternisation by the German crews, which unfortunately took place despite the exhortations of the German officers, evoked no response.

During the time of our stay in the Firth of Forth a more or less thick bank of fog hid most of our ships from the eyes of the English public. Few excursion steamers showed themselves. The English public, so far as we could understand in the flagship, kept quiet about it and restrained themselves; only one 'lady,' who passed us by raised her fist in anger.

The outward show of anxiety by the English over the poor protection of our anchorage against easterly gales was extraordinary. However, they put this anxiety well in the foreground when pressure was brought to bear to move the

German ships as soon as possible to a more sheltered harbour. It was quite true to say that the anchorage afforded little shelter against easterly gales, but this was known beforehand; a more enclosed anchorage, therefore (e.g. Scapa Flow), would have served for this inspection. Yet it is not the principle of English politics to do anything clumsily; England knows by long experience that she should be more kind to people than to dogs and cut off their tails bit by bit instead of all at once. Removal to a more sheltered port – Scapa Flow was selected – indicating a further docking of the naval 'tail' from the German people's body. The demand for the transfer of the German fleet to the Firth of Forth was recognised as the first step in the betrayal, which we have set out to prove, and this closely followed by the second and third steps; the journey to Scapa Flow and the internment.

The English commander-in-chief had sent a wireless message to the German commander-in-chief on the 20th November, informing him that the steamers for bringing back the surplus members of the ships' companies were to be sent to Scapa Flow. The squadron command did not know of this wireless signal as it was not intercepted by the *Friedrich der Grosse*. Not until the 22nd November did we know for certain where our next port of call was to be. Two English orders, dated 22nd and 23rd November, came to hand regarding formation, course, action in fog, during the transit through the Pentland Skerries[7] and for anchoring at Scapa Flow. The latter confirmed the order of the fleet for the transfer from Wilhelmshaven and Kiel. The torpedo boats started on the 22nd November. On the 24th the large cruisers followed, on the 25th November the Fourth Squadron, on the 26th November the last ships left the Firth of Forth. At 12 noon on the 25th November the Fourth Squadron weighed anchor and steamed in misty, and later, thick foggy weather from the Firth of Forth. Our escort consisted of the English flagship, the battleship *Emperor of India*, which took station in the van as guide, and four more battleships, of which two took station to port and two to starboard. One ship would have been ample to guide us through the English minefields, but it suited the English design that through this strict supervision they would, bit by bit, accustom us to the fact that we had been captured by England in battle.

The next morning we ran into the bay of Scapa Flow through a triple boom defence of hawsers and spars, and provisionally anchored in the northwestern part. Later on an English officer came on board to lead each ship singly to its final anchorage further westward. About midday the *Friedrich der Grosse* was somewhere near her appointed anchorage after two abortive attempts to reach it. The other ships had equally little success. If only the English officers had been permitted to disclose the positions of the anchorage to our officers, the anchoring, which in such undisturbed waters was no great feat of art, would certainly have taken only half the time.

CHAPTER II

Interned in Scapa Flow – first reduction of crews – considerations of the position – my journey home

The bay of Scapa Flow is enclosed by seven large and small islands of the Orkneys group. The basin is roomy. Several narrow channels join it to the sea. The terrific and extraordinarily strong currents outside are hardly noticeable inside the bight. The islands are mountainous and rocky. The lower parts of the land showed signs of rude cultivation. Trees and shrubs were nowhere to be seen; most of it was covered in heather, out of which stuck the naked rock. Several fishing villages were just in sight on land in the far distance – apart from which here and there on the coast stood unfriendly-looking farmhouses built of the grey local stone. Several military works, such as barracks, aeroplane sheds or balloon hangars, relieved the monotonous sameness; in ugliness they would beat even ours at a bet. A meteorological station adorns the top of one of the many hills. Due to the influence of the Gulf Stream the weather is very changeable. During the winter heavy storms are the rule; except for one at Christmas-time we escaped them, whereas on the other hand small storms occurred quite frequently. The climate is extraordinarily bracing, never very cold and never very warm. The bay is well suited as an exercising area for warships due to its roominess and sheltered waters. It makes a forbidding and grim impression on the visitor.

The German ships and torpedo boats were anchored or lying at buoys about the small island of Cava in the southwesterly part of the bay. An English squadron and destroyer flotilla remained stationed in the bight to guard them, the former lay at anchor east of Cava about three miles from us, the latter close to our own torpedo boats. A collection of armed drifters and fishing boats, which cruised round our ships day and night, showed what a close watch was being kept. They scrutinised the German ships and reported at once if any irregularity appeared to be taking place. Even the thickening of smoke from a funnel would raise their suspicions.

These stifling measures of supervision and security made every man of the ships' crews realise that the gate to freedom, to the journey to a neutral port and to the return to the Homeland was firmly closed.

Without much prompting from outside the name of the squadron from being the 'Squadron to be led over to the Firth of Forth,' became the 'Scapa Flow Interned Squadron.'

That the German Government could or wished to dispute this fact was not apparent, as she had renounced 'Might' as a foreign policy and substituted 'Right' in its stead. For the interned squadron there only remained this fact and the sad consequences to reckon with and to prepare itself for a long stay at Scapa Flow. The replenishment and next supply of provisions, tobacco, soap, clothing, and money, had to be arranged and regulated. The supply of

39

provisions, tobacco, and soap, to which England was bound, of course against payment, was refused, although the blockade of Germany, which still held good, was taken into consideration. These essentials of life had to be brought from Wilhelmshaven. Due to the initially unfavourable means of getting them over many of these valuable things were lost. As soon as a steamer, at the instigation of the squadron, was detailed for this duty and came over regularly once a month, order and honesty were attained in the supply. The post and passenger service was maintained direct with the Homeland by a light cruiser or a torpedo boat. They ran once a week to collect and deliver mails to Scapa Flow. At that time the mails were not censored by the English authorities. The direct delivery of wireless messages was forbidden us; they had to be turned over to the English admiral on the spot to be forwarded.

We lacked coal, water, oil, materials and gear of all sorts sufficient to keep us ready for sea. Coal and water were supplied by England, against payment, everything else had to be brought over from Wilhelmshaven. The utmost meanness in these things had to be fought against by the squadron.

In the condition of readiness for sea that the ships were in, the last glimmer of hope, that we should once again turn our backs on the captivity of Scapa Flow, was snuffed out. We also put forward to our enemies the written legal claim in the Armistice undertaking, which we on no occasion wished to see violated, that contrary to truth and honesty the ships were to be allowed to fall into disrepair. The state of readiness for sea of the material was well kept, up to the last days before the sinking, and the state of readiness of the personnel up to within a few days of this, against all attempts at opposition.

The German ships' companies were forbidden any dialogue by the English between their own ships or with the English crews and were forbidden to go ashore. There was little opportunity for communication with the English. The English dispatch boats bringing the mails did not come alongside, they used to come just close enough not to drop the bags into the water and throw them on board as they sheered past. The English dispatch boats only lay alongside the flagship during the mornings. Here soon, by reason of a prolific growth of trade in barter, a way was broken for a real dialogue between the two enemy countries and, as in the later course of the internment the strict orders of the English were somewhat relaxed, it came occasionally to pass that individual guard-boats went alongside German ships at night and carried on a trade with the crews.[8]

Whether this barter by night, which seemed somewhat questionable, was not somehow organised by the English admiral himself, to get an idea of our nightly activities and to win over our crews by spirituous commerce, I am not certain. There was no reason to oppose this trade in barter, as it was only to be wished for that the enormous quantity of brandy should be reduced and thereby increase in value.

The efforts of the English to prevent any fraternisation between our crews and theirs as much as possible showed that they themselves were none too sure of the loyalty of their own ships' companies. We learned through the English press and from the stories of the drifters' crews that waves of unrest to the prejudice of discipline were passing through their fleet and that only by timely and indiscriminate shooting of agitators[†] had this been kept down. The lower English ratings showed a definite interest and curiosity; they appeared to have approached the squadron Soldiers' Council delegates and listened to the detailing of their revolutionary organisation and to what advantage they had gained by their struggles. The English crews were at that time claiming a rise in pay. The English Government did not consider the combined demand of the lower grades of the navy personnel to be quite so harmless as it appeared, as it at once doubled the pay of men and officers without having obtained previous parliamentary sanction.

When it became clear that the English order against fraternisation was due in the first place to the fear that the Germans might spread their revolutionary propaganda amongst the English fleet and people, the motive for the idea that the German crews should be made to feel that they were prisoners, instead of being interned, was also evident. This type of unworthy and disdainful treatment, which was contrary to every usual international custom, was meant to show England in the full glory of the judgment of the world and to degrade the German seamen before the English people and before the whole world. They tried to impart a particular brilliance to this glorification by inviting a great number of dignitaries and representatives of the press to view the fleet.

The forbidding of communication between German ships due to the revolutionary propaganda, which was still cultivated by some of the German ships' crews, especially the baiting of officers, was not found to be entirely oppressive by the squadron command, as it served in this way to help in the maintenance of discipline and order when required. I felt the sense of humiliation against the foregoing with every single member of the crews, at the denial of shore leave. We needed this to keep body and soul healthy. I never tired in again and again attempting to get permission for this. The local naval commanders were not against it personally, but were refused by the Admiralty in London, and they had to stand by this refusal as a matter of principle.

At my request I, personally, was allowed to inspect the various ships under my orders between the hours of 10 a.m. and 3 p.m., using my own barge for these visits, though I still had to submit the names of the ships to be visited to the English beforehand. This permission was later extended to the officers of my staff. The intervention of the Head Soldiers' Councillor, who had smuggled his delegates into my barge as the crew in order to exercise a personal and mostly mutinous influence on the other ships, later compelled me to use an English dispatch boat instead of my barge for visits of inspection. Later on it was permitted to bring individual captains and ships' officers on board my flagship

[†]Von Reuter's reference to indescriminate shooting is, in fact, not true. The British newspapers were no less sensational then than they are today, and while there was unrest in the Royal Navy the Admiralty never resorted to such draconian measures.

after notice had been given. I was able to keep personal contact with my officers and men in different spheres through these concessions.

In accordance with the Armistice conditions ship-keepers were to be detailed to remain aboard the ships and torpedo craft and the surplus portions of the crews were to be sent back to the Homeland.

The proposals of the German commander-in-chief on the subject of the strength of the care and maintenance parties appeared to the English commander-in-chief to have been set at too high a figure. On the 23rd November he gave the following basis to be worked on to the German commander-in-chief:

"The total numbers in the care and maintenance parties to be left on board the interned ships, including officers, must not exceed the following: battleships 175, battlecruisers 200, light cruisers 60, torpedo craft 20. These numbers exceed by a considerable amount the totals that would be required in British ships of similar classes, and can therefore be still further reduced as found necessary later on. The repatriation of all, except the numbers shown above, must be prepared for at once. Inform me of the earliest date on which the transports can sail."

The squadron command had requested the ships to understand and announced that the most important point was that at all times the ships should be ready to steam at 10 knots, so that they could steam at this speed to neutral ports or Wilhelmshaven, or in the case of accident, e.g. parting of cables in a gale, they would be able to manoeuvre. Of course, the demands of heat, light, care and maintenance of engines and boilers had to be taken into consideration, with the number of hands available. The officers who were to remain behind were: aboard battleships and heavy cruisers, one junior staff officer or senior lieutenant-commander as captain, two executive officers, two assistant engineers, one medical officer, one administrative officer; on board light cruisers, a senior lieutenant-commander as captain, one executive officer, one assistant engineer, one medical officer, and one administrative officer. The leader of the torpedo craft was to give the necessary orders for his flotilla. Even my staff was rigorously reduced. Apart from the battlecruisers and torpedo boats, who requested for a slight increase in strength, the units of the squadron agreed with the numbers laid down by the English. My very small request for a slight increase in these numbers was refused in a verbal interview with the English naval commander, although I had expected all along that my proposals would not be accepted. A definite object, which we could not see through clearly, was apparently kept in mind by Admiral Beatty, which seemed so important to the admiral on the spot that he thought himself constrained to refuse our proposals for the very slightest increase in numbers.

The care and maintenance parties were not established on board the ships and torpedo boats without friction. The surplus personnel, several thousands in number, were preparing for their journey home; everywhere on board busy activity ruled, clear of politics. The home-going transports that had been detailed kept us waiting.

Although only a few weeks had gone by since I took over the leadership of the squadron, the period had already been full of achievements and impressions. I had gained a correct perspective and, relying on this, could be clear on the points of view and the lines on which the interned squadron should be led. My object was, henceforward, to preserve this assembled portion of the High Seas Fleet for the German State, whose property it was.

It was unbelievable to me that the Entente would appropriate our ships, even formally (after they had made quite certain of theirs in the fastness of Scapa Flow during the war!), without producing very valid reasons for the step. These reasons might arise externally, for instance, if the war were to break out again, or internally, if the orders given by the English to the interned squadron were not complied with. Again, they might arise if grave disorders or excesses on board by the revolutionary crews led to the disregard of their officers, whom the English regarded as the supporters of discipline and order, and who were made responsible for the carrying out of the English regulations.

I could rule out the external contingency, as it was inadmissible that the German Government would allow of a resumption of hostilities; all signs pointed too openly against it. By my estimate of their character I took it also to be out of the question that they would resist the appropriation of the fleet for an internal reason; they would not have gone further than a single protest. I have not been able to rid myself of the idea that the government had already given up the interned squadron at the time of the Armistice; their conduct at the Armistice negotiations and their acquiescence at the detention of the German ships at Scapa Flow all point to this. It therefore appeared to me that the preservation of our possession of the ships was placed entirely in the hands of the commander of the interned squadron.

In order to defend our right of possession, it was essential to let the enemy understand that we held firmly and unconditionally to our ships. This could be done by keeping our ships and torpedo boats in a state of readiness for steaming and by emphasising our views should any attempts be made against them. A proof of our right of possession lay in the fact that the English had left us to fly our command flags - pendants and admiral's flag - and had just as much left to me the higher jurisdiction which was entailed in my appointment by the High Seas Fleet, and this had not been disputed on the English side. Jurisdiction is the sign of sovereignty; this was therefore left to me despite the internment. I could admit no deviation from the last two standpoints.

In order to keep the ships in our possession we had to follow the English regulations. This could only be done by the officers again taking full charge of the men and by the re-establishment of their authority. The Soldiers' Council delegates, with their radical adherents, would not only bitterly oppose these endeavours, but would fight them, even to the knife. In this way serious disorders might arise and by laying aside the authority of the officers, endanger our right of tenure of the ships. Might and right, to put aside the Soldiers' Councillors or to render them impotent, were lacking. This vicious circle counselled foresight and caution. When might fails to guide the path of evolution in a given direction, we must arm ourselves with patience and wait for opportunities; eagerly awaited opportunities come to pass of themselves. One must then, only be able to recognise them, to seize them vigorously and not shrink from any fights or conflicts. It seemed to be the easier course - in the interests of our right of tenure - not to create any trouble until the required opportunity arose, and if once begun not to allow it to grow to too large a dimension.

However much it was to be wished for, to instruct the officers of the squadron in my aims and the methods of achieving them, this could not be carried out because of my isolation from my ships and because of the unbelievable mistrust of the men in the activities of the officers, whose every step they watched, and using any unusual occurrence as a pretext for unruliness. The letter post was also under the secret watch of the radical elements so that messages by this channel, as soon as they contained anything except on a subject of indifference to them, went irremediably amiss. This censorship had, amongst other things, compelled me also to forgo the sending of any written reports to the authorities at home. Our correspondence outwards and in the squadron itself, following the saying of Talleyrand[9]: 'A written word - and I bring the man to the gallows,' was reduced to a bare minimum and what was left divorced from any semblance of politics. The reticence in correspondence laid on us the pleasant compulsion of always telling the truth. We were careful to instruct our memories; facts remain in the mind, lies disappear. In this way we avoided getting inextricably involved in traps by keeping a sharp look out.

Luckily I could renew my hopes of bringing my officers into the picture. The preparations for the journey home provisionally occupied the attention of the crews. After the reduction, which left only a small number on board, through which many minor dissensions were bound to fan away, the old order between officers and men might possibly re-establish itself of its own accord. In this, however, I was badly mistaken. Thus it came to pass, later on, in the first months after the reduction, that the revolutionary elements and agitators directed their attentions almost entirely on the fleet command and that trouble actually broke out on board the flagship. Thus I got the conclusive counter measures into my hands.

In that connection how that agent of the English Government, the Admiralty in London, and the local English commander at Scapa Flow, would act was still obscure.

It was to be expected from the Admiralty that they would be guided solely by the interests of England and that they would not allow us to extract ourselves by a so-called sympathy for our position or any other knightly feeling. The interests of England then lay: to make certain of the watch on the interned squadron at the least expense, to prepare and smooth the way for the taking over of the squadron by the English or the Entente with no great stir either through some particular occurrence or by the conclusion of peace and, finally, through the resumption of hostilities, the seizure of the ships to make them harmless to the Entente.

The English Admiralty must have known that on board the German ships the relationship between officers and men was rather strained. In accordance with the popular English system it was just this tension which had to be fostered in order to keep the two opposing parties in a state of equilibrium without waste of strength or money. Should the equilibrium be disturbed by the greater weight of one party, they had only to add a little weight to the rising scale, through their admiral at Scapa Flow, for a state of equilibrium to be re-established. The local English naval commander of the guard ships would have liked the course of affairs to follow this line. His support could therefore be relied on to add to the weight of the officers, if need be, but only within the boundaries set to keep a state of equilibrium and never beyond them. The knowledge of these boundaries had the effect of restraining me from seeking the support of the English to re-establish the authority of my officers. It was also repugnant to me in my own mind to rely on others, particularly hostile-minded ones, rather than on myself. In this connection I could very well foresee a case - foreign politics that I could not attempt to review at Scapa Flow might bring one up at any moment - by which the very fact of my going to the English admiral for support would supply the long-wished-for pretext to the Entente for the seizure of the ships.

During the further course of the internment at Scapa Flow it appeared at times that the English admiral was ready to take over completely our authority from us. This did not fail in influencing me not to rely on the English admiral. I have, however, never seen him make a greater effort than that needed to balance the officers' side of the scale which he perhaps rated at a higher weight than it in reality was, with that of our revolutionary opponents in the squadron; it is possible, though, that this was through the fear that the disorderly conduct of the Germans would have an effect on his own ships' companies. In any case, I withstood all encouragement and temptations to lean on the English admiral for support. That did not, however, prevent me from using him on occasion, indirectly out of the respect that was due to him as the representative of the unscrupulous English might, to counter the evil-minded amongst those serving under me.

I kept to the principle, in all my dealings and actions, of keeping my attention directed on the English Admiralty - they always had the last word in any decision. They took us officers and, since the war, the revolutionaries in the fleet, to be the hostile working elements in the minds of the Entente. In any case, it appeared to me better to maintain a frankly hostile attitude towards them rather than a precariously friendly one. It seemed to me wiser, in order not to imperil our ownership of the ships, to conceal any disorders from the English admiral or to let them appear harmless, so as to restrain him from seizure of the squadron - still one had not to overlook the fact that such a thing might go too far and thus precipitate a most unforeseen situation, which, solely on the grounds by which the English lay such a store, might get irrevocably out of hand.

I thought that the legal prosecution of English methods would serve best in the view that the English admiral at Scapa Flow should be kept at a distance; further, it also seemed favourable to break a way for a trusted relationship towards him.

The more confidence I was able to win personally, the more could I expect not to be interfered with and supervised. In this way I kept the possibility of being able to settle disturbances without outward stir and render them sterile. I had also to strengthen my position in the tolerable relationship towards the English admiral whilst the radical elements in the squadron tended to worsen it by lording it over me. I had my choice ready of which attitude I should assume towards the English naval commander and towards the Head Soldiers' Councillor. The leader of the soldiers' council had informed me, a few days after our arrival at Scapa Flow, that the first steps towards fraternisation had been taken towards him by the English petty officers and men and asked whether he should now distribute the necessary propaganda for the incitement of the English fleet to mutiny. The proposal was at first very tempting, but did not bear close scrutiny. I could not credit his news with any good intentions, nor did the propaganda promise any great following. The victory of their system of government stood too clearly before the eyes of the English ships' companies by the internment of the German fleet; the pride in their land and government would have been stronger than any leaning towards internationalism, pacifism, and such very un-English actions. Above all these considerations, however, my feelings as an officer warned me to have only the bare minimum of dealings with the radical elements. Their way of thinking and their actions had proved not to be bound by any sort of code of morals, so that they had to be treated with the deepest distrust. We officers had nothing in common with the revolution, and we wished to have nothing in common with those whose doings had plunged our land in immeasurable sorrow and deepest shame. So I forbade propaganda.

It seemed important to me to have an appreciation of how the English would behave in the case of disorders taking place. I had already put out a feeler. The answer did not quite please me. My question was probably misinterpreted; it became involved with the question of the loyalty of the officers, which was never in question. I would never have approached the English admiral on this account. In order to make it appear that this question was not urgent I provisionally allowed the matter to drop.

A list of questions, which would have better been talked over between the English admiral and myself, delayed its settlement.

The leader of the torpedo boat flotilla had informed me that during the search of the ships in the Firth of Forth, English officers had expressed the opinion that the German officers of the squadron were more or less thought to be revolutionaries as well. They had based this view on the grounds of the fact that we officers, in mutual agreement with the mutinous crews, had led the ships over to the Firth of Forth. I did not want to leave this stigma on the officers. It happened by sheer good fortune that Admiral Madden, who had informed me in the Firth of Forth that I could seek a meeting with him at any time, was on guard with his squadron at Scapa Flow. I now requested a conference and it was arranged for the 27th November. In company with my chief of staff and with a staff officer as interpreter I went on board the English flagship. I opened the conversation by bringing unambiguously forward the fact that we officers had nothing in common with the revolutionary crews, and refused any familiarity with them. The reasons which moved us to take a part in the transfer of the squadron had been to maintain peace and order in the German State, to guard our country against even greater misfortunes than the sorry state to which the revolution had brought us. At the conclusion of my statements Admiral Madden answered: "I understand your position."

The following subjects were then discussed:

1. The reduction of the crews and the number of hands in the care and maintenance parties. My proposals were taken into consideration, but they remained, as previously related, unheeded.

2. Responsibility for the seaworthiness of the ships. This depended on the strength of the care and maintenance parties. As this strength was settled by the English, the English Government was then bound to take over this responsibility. For certain reasons I retained the responsibility for their seaworthiness so as to retain my independence from the English admiral in my leadership of the squadron. It was apparently left to me as it was before. Distress signals were to be given me.

3. Shore leave. I sought to have the previous written orders on the subject altered, so that permission would be granted to the crews for shore going. I would not agree to a one-sided arrangement of leave for officers only. Requests to the Admiralty were set in motion. Their decision would be forwarded to me later.

4. Commissariat. I dwelt on the badly provisioned state of the ships and asked for help as necessary. Although I had called attention to a promise of Admiral Beatty that he would not let the German crews starve, the question still remained unsettled. A wireless message sent to the commander-in-chief High Seas Fleet by Admiral Madden without my knowledge, ordering provisions to be sent, demonstrated the way in which Admiral Beatty was endeavouring to guard us from starvation.

During these negotiations, as well as at the later ones, I spoke German; my remarks were translated into English by an English interpreter, and vice versa. What the English admiral said was translated for me into German. The formality that was observed toward me was of a cold nature, but it was not without a certain courtliness.

The first two transports, the *Sierra Ventana* and the *Graf Waldersee*, for the repatriation of the surplus members of the crews, arrived at Scapa Flow on the 3rd December. Four more followed, in pairs, a few days later. On the 13th December the last home-going transports left Scapa Flow. I joined this party on board the steamer *Bremen*.

As I have already related, I wanted to return to the Homeland after the squadron had been interned, as there did not appear to be any further field of activity for me once the working for the organisation of the care and maintenance parties had been arranged. I had taken the necessary steps for this immediately after our arrival at Scapa Flow. In the further course of the internment it was more and more apparent that an admiral in command of the squadron, and under the direct supervision of the Navy Office, was unnecessary. I could scarcely hope to succeed by merely written representations all the way from Scapa Flow. To put in a personal appearance at home seemed to me to be imperative. My journey home was therefore synonymous with my retirement from the leadership of the squadron. I would rather that this could have been avoided as I had meanwhile grown accustomed to my work and had found a circle of willing helpers. I was therefore glad when, on the 11th December, the two wireless messages, shown below, reached me, which made my return to Scapa Flow possible. The text is given here again as they are yet noteworthy in another sense, in that this well-meaning telegram of the Armistice Commission tacitly acknowledged, though unintentionally of course, their apparent acquiescence in the internment of the German fleet at Scapa Flow. Paragraph 3 was unnecessary, as no censorship existed. The answer of the English commander-in-chief avoids going into the principal question which is in paragraph 1, and is chiefly remarkable for the manner in which he thought to settle the German demands.

Wireless message from WAKO [Watch Command].

'The terms in Article 23 of the Armistice conditions lay down, in the first place, that an internment of German ships in neutral ports must be accepted. Contrary to the clear meaning of these terms the ships' companies (care and maintenance parties) of the interned ships are being treated as prisoners-of-war in the English ports.

I therefore request, first of all, that the following regulations come into force at once:

1. The care and maintenance parties will not be treated as prisoners-of-war, and in consequence accelerated postal service including German newspapers without censorship.
2. Confirmed leave conditions for going home by permission of

commanding officers, and free travelling facilities for this purpose.

3. The quickest possible establishment of an uncensored postal service.'

(Signed) Goette, Vizeadmiral.

To this the English commander-in-chief made the following reply on the 11th December:

'Leave for officers and men to travel back to Germany will be continued in so far as German transport facilities and general circumstances warrant.'

I was therefore only taking leave to go to Germany and the next senior officer, Commodore Dominik, took over my duties.

During the time I was collecting the opinions of the crews regarding sending home the surplus numbers I had no thought at any time of leaving the squadron for good.

Once back at home I transmitted my proposals to the then Deputy Secretary of State for the Government Navy Office for the placing of the squadron directly under his orders. The business on this subject and on one or two other untoward points delayed my return to Scapa Flow. It was not till the 25th January that I got back there.

CHAPTER III

**Again at Scapa Flow - protest of the government against the internment -
The radical crews and the authority of the officers - The Red Guard and
discipline - purging of the Soldiers' Council**

During my absence at the end of December, for no apparent reason, a
censorship of our out-going mails had been established. Further, at the end of
January the Armistice Commission had addressed a strong protest to the
Entente, at the instigation of the Secretary of State for the Navy Office, against
the retention of the German ships in internment at Scapa Flow. This would
perhaps have worked more impressively had the German Government been
able to decide not to let the battleship *Baden* put out until the subject of the
protest had been settled. So the protest was not answered at all. The fact that
there was no answer fettered the German Government. I had the feeling that
the protest, however earnest it was meant to be by the Navy Office, was only
intended by the government to save its face. This indeed was how it was
understood by the Entente.

What sadly disturbed me on my return, above all else, was that the change in
the internal situation in the ships did not appear to have led altogether to a re-
establishment of orderly conduct and loyal discipline. Considerable disorders
had taken place, amongst others, while the commanding officer of the flagship
was away for a matter of an hour or two and had left a warrant officer in charge.
The Head Soldier's delegate of the day was replaced by one who was even more
radical; further, a collection of men amounting to about a fifth of the crew of
the flagship, under the leadership of a 'Spartakist' minded leading stoker, had
formed themselves into a Red Guard.

The internment was fruitful ground for the growth of unrest. The isolation
from the outside world and the spiritually monotonous and physically easy
round of duty, which left them plenty of time to themselves, had considerably
increased their desire for the sensational. The wireless news, the press, and
letters, with their accounts of the street fighting which had occurred during
January 1919, in Berlin and other parts of Germany, but particularly the news
of the death of Liebknecht and Rosa Luxemburg[10], had evoked universal
excitement. From this attitude of mind a strong resentment had grown up
against all persons, who, the masses took for granted, did not understand their
exaggerated desires and would refuse and hinder them; the officers were, of
course, reckoned on being the chief of those in opposition to them.

The majority of the crews thought themselves well entitled to unusual
privileges. They lived in the belief that with the transfer over of the ships and
the taking over of the internment responsibility by the government, they had
proved of the utmost service and, indeed, as they no longer considered
themselves liable for military duties they merely carried on voluntarily. They
waited to be singled out before all the rest of the personnel of the navy, in

keeping with the spirit of the times, for a special reward.

Through letters from home one learned that the conditions for the men had been enormously bettered without any consideration having been given to the interned ships' companies. Many of the men felt themselves to have been deceived, abandoned, and degraded. The political agitators had fostered this grievance and had used it, as far as necessary, to depose the Head Soldiers' Councillor whom they did not consider active enough and replace him by a new one who knew what to aim for. Further, a committee formed by the most radically-minded men and sent with the errand to the Secretary of State for the Navy Office in Berlin, there to push through their financial and political ideas, to fulfilment. These are said to be the minutes which were taken of the oral discussion which was conducted in the Reich Naval Office:

Demands of the Delegation	*Decisions of the Secretary of State.*
1. The recognition of the Head Soldiers' Councillor of the interned fleet.	1. The Head Soldiers' Councillor is recognised as he is designated in accordance with the Central Council of the German Republic for the exercise of the judicial authority.
2. The retention of Soldiers' Councils on board the interned ships until they return home or until the return of the crews.	2. The Soldiers' Councils may remain as may be found necessary for the exercise of their authority. In this connection it is to be noted: (a) For each ship the committee shall consist of a maximum of three delegates. (b) For each torpedo boat flotilla until further notice 10 to 12 boats, one committee of a maximum of three delegates.
3. Members of the crews of the interned ships only to be relieved of their duty with the consent of the Head Soldiers' Councillor of the interned squadron.	3. It will be understood that the extraordinary position due to the numbers of the crews being reduced to barely sufficient strength must be taken into consideration. The station commander will be instructed to keep the local authorities in the interned squadron informed of any impending important changes in personnel, and he will draw up a scheme to this effect.
4. (Immaterial)	4. (Immaterial: not dealt with.)
5. Installation of an 'interned party' at Wilhelmshaven so that supplies can be guaranteed. Recall of a representative from the interned squadron to take charge of it.	5. As a party for the interned squadron already exists in Wilhelmshaven, there is no objection to a representative of the interned squadron being detailed on the grounds of the extraordinary situation in Scapa Flow, to go there. For this object a suitable representative

6. That in the retention of a People's Navy, the first consideration will be given to the professional soldier element in the interned squadron.

7. Stabilisation of the emoluments of the short and active service personnel:
(a) Pay and allowances as before, in addition 'interned money' for men, officers, and officials, at the rate of 5 marks a day, payable as from the 21 November.

(b) A gratuity on discharge for civilian clothes.

(c) Confirmation of leave of absence, including pay and allowances, for four weeks on return.
(d) Increase of the victualling allowance by half a mark a day, and the serving out of 'mess savings' that have been withheld up to date.

from the ships of the interned squadron may be selected. There is no objection to a representative travelling in the link ships to turn over orders and to watch over their safe delivery.

6. It is a matter of course that the members of the professional personnel in the interned squadron who do their duty will be given every and full consideration; that they in all cases should receive particular consideration above all others cannot be considered in view of economic reasons. But it is confirmed that this matter will be kept in mind.

7.

(a) Pay and allowances as before. From the 1st January onwards an addition of 2 marks will be paid daily to all men, including warrant officers, at the same time a single gratuity of 225 marks will be payable for the part taken by them in transfer over of the fleet.
(b) Discharge money and clothes will be continued in accordance with the regulations.
(c) Agreed provided the internment lasts at least four months.

(d) From the 1st February onwards the crews of the interned ships will be paid half a mark more victualling money than the rate of victualling allowance in force at home. The free issue of the mess savings, which originated in the years 1914-1915, cannot now continue on its old footing, as these savings arose in consequence of the establishment of too high a rate of victualling allowance, and not through a reduction in the victuals supplied to the men.

Approved.
Berlin, 24th January 1919
Signed.

The interned squadron was neither interested in these proceedings nor did it have any knowledge of the claims set out above. It need hardly be stated that the committee were not empowered or authorised to put forward demands in the names of officers, as they had done in paragraph 7 (a).

Parallel to these efforts aimed at economic advantage ran strong currents of politics. They arose out of a desire to keep the forces of 'reaction' at a distance. They were afraid of being robbed of the 'fruits of the revolution' by these forces, that is, to lose the personal and financial advantages, which the proletariat, to which one was answerable, had obtained by a struggle at the expense of the public. The officer appeared to them to embody the spirit of reaction. The fight was aimed at him. These ideas guided the actions of the Head Soldiers' Councillor and the many radically-minded Soldiers' Councils in the ships and were urged on them by their following amongst the men whose creed it was. They would never admit the reinstatement of the officers in their former predominating and unassailable position. They would have preferred to dispense with the officer altogether; but this could not he obtained as in the eyes of the English admiral the officer was the representative of the squadron and of the ships, to which official position - much to their chagrin - they were debarred by the English admiral and, because of his professional knowledge, in which the great majority recognised the only safeguard for their safety on board, the officer was seen to be indispensable. In this way the radical elements had to put up with the continued presence of the officers, though they made efforts to make the officers subordinate to themselves and to make them merely their tools.

Apart from the interests of caste the certain retention of our rights of possession of the ships demanded that the officer should be reinstated in his old position towards the men in order to re-establish his authority. The aims of the officers and of the Soldiers' Councils were bitterly opposed. The establishment of the Soldiers' Councils could not be disregarded as it was ordered by the proceedings of the 24th January to continue until the end of the internment. Besides legal remedies, the power to uproot this harmful decision was also absent. So a means had to be sought by which the radicals might be displaced from the unassailable position they had held until now. This aim could only be entirely realised if we succeeded in helping the small number of loyal petty officers and men to a greater influence and in winning back the majority to regarding the officer in a trustworthy light. By means of new elections better-minded delegates for the Soldiers' Councils might then perhaps be won, and it might be - in favourable circumstances - that the men themselves would express the wish to give up the establishment of Soldiers' Councils.

To increase the influence of the loyal sailors much was done by the leader of the torpedo craft and one or two energetic and fortunately-placed commanders. In this connection Kapitänleutnant Elze of the *Emden* must be especially mentioned. A party began to form in the squadron, which at once offered opposition to the activities of the radical Soldiers' Councils. It gained force somewhat in the torpedo craft, in two or three cruisers and in two battleships.

Contrary to this, the signs of winning over the greater part of the men seemed unfavourable. In their efforts to gain confidence the officers must have been in a very difficult position. Their confidence was entirely governed by their ruling thoughts at the time and the desire for economic gain. Whoever provided them with the most, or even only just promised it, had their confidence. In this connection the radical is in an easy position, as he does not feel bound to fight against economic advantage on moral grounds; he has, and holds, the confidence of the masses. The officer in his idealism, on the other hand, feels himself bound to consider the good of the State, to be answerable to the whole people; he is not in a position to suppress harmful economic struggles. There lies the great insurmountable weakness of his position, its tragedy, that he, in times like the present, governed by economic stresses, unlike former days when knightly thoughts still moved the people, can place himself as champion at the head of the agitation. He must from his point of view as an officer fight against this new agitation, led as it is by this economic aim. Yet it will just be this fight that will lose him the confidence of the masses. These considerations were but little expected by me on the part of the masses. It were better to attempt to strengthen the position of the officers by the separation and sending home of those of the men who were tending to follow the new economic ideas of the radicals. Of course, such sendings home to a great extent and, on the other hand, hindrances and reductions, rather put it out of the question to attempt to keep the state of readiness for sea of the personnel up to the necessary mark.

The revival of the authority of the officers would also serve the higher jurisdiction that I had requested at the beginning and had now been assigned to me. Co-operation with the Soldiers' Councils was excluded from this; in this way I had at least a shadow of right to my hand, which was the only one at my disposal. In January I could still award punishments for infractions of discipline. Permission for such a thing had come from the ship's company, which wanted a certain amount of order and security of personal property. The lawyer of the squadron had modified the punishment orders, which had been upset by the revolution and placed at the will of the men. The punishments of arrest, whose award and execution on land was met with much opposition and which was not altogether possible, were replaced by money fines or done away with altogether. The new disciplinary punishment code was held in universal esteem by high and low and the men accustomed themselves again to the idea that infractions of discipline were to be atoned for by punishments. After the installation of the new government the earlier punishment code, which did not mention fines, was brought into force again. The Navy Office would not promise to leave the squadron their code as it was. I therefore had no option but to put into force the code that had been accepted before the revolution. The result was that punishments were only awarded on board ships whose general conduct allowed it. The award and execution of a cell punishment on board a battleship, which did not meet with general approval, led to serious rioting, which at least jeopardised our right of ownership of the ships. My higher jurisdiction, which had been safeguarded until then, disappeared with

54

the change of code. Not only was my authority in the squadron weakened by this course of action, the only apparent sign of its sovereignty was imperilled. Eventually I succeeded in inducing the Navy Office to give me back these powers in spite of themselves, on the grounds of the re-establishment of my jurisdiction.

Naturally, we could not rigidly adopt one or the other means of raising the position of the officers due to the complicated nature of the service with which we had to grapple and the shrinkage in the strength of the crews, but rather that everything which tended towards it should be fostered and used. In the further course of the internment the position did indeed better itself; we were successful in obtaining delegates true to the navy and State as Head Soldiers' Councillor and also a few other councillors. Still we could not gain a sufficient following to throw out the influence of the radicals. The sinking was the first sign in the change of tone for the upholding of government, Fatherland, and officers.

I must not let it go unrecorded that a number of warrant officers, petty officers, and men maintained their loyalty in their personal intercourse with their officers in the way that was usual before the revolution in spite of all threats and intimidation. Especially so was the conduct of the junior ratings of my staff; well indeed did the signal personnel, under the leadership of the excellent senior petty officer, shed the light of their assiduity and devotedness to duty over all the other ships and thereby ensured that the whole of the signal organisation of the squadron worked smoothly. The admirable sentiments of the members of my staff are one of the few pleasant memories I retain of my period of command at Scapa Flow.

In order to raise the contentment of the men, I put a request before the local English naval commander that he should seek by personal interview to have the orders for the forbidden shore leave and for the censorship of our letters rescinded; there were also other requests, but of less importance, which I mentioned to him. During the course of the conversation it transpired that on the subject of authorising the shore leave the English admiral himself had nothing against it, but still he would first have to ask the Admiralty. As I knew what the views of the Admiralty were, I knew perfectly well that the suggestion would again be refused. Concerning the censorship of the mails he proposed to meet my request by installing the censor's office on board one of his own ships. This arrangement had the result of establishing the censor's office shortly afterwards, but unfortunately it also soon came to an end, at least for private correspondence.

I sought, further, for an English dispatch boat to attend on me on the routine visits to my ships, as to my regret I could not be certain that my barge would not be used by others behind my back and unknown to the English. The request was granted.

Finally, I once again obtained the confirmation of the fact, from the English admiral, that for his part the Soldiers' Councillors did not exist and that he would have no dealings with them.

Matters came quickly to a head at the beginning of February through demonstrations on board my flagship by the Red Guard. The serving out of alcohol was forced. The repellent state of affairs induced by the liberal issues of spirits was treated with disapproval by the better part of the crew. The stopping of the issue of spirits was imminent; the last straw was when a petty officer, newly returned from Wilhelmshaven with his lurid Spartakist portrayal of the situation at home, greatly excited the ship's company. As a result there arose a quite understandable difference of opinion between the radicals and the better elements. In order to assure myself of the attitude of the English admiral in the event of this difference of opinion coming to blows, and if our right of possession would be jeopardised by such a conflict, I informed him of my intended visit. The unusual time of day at which this occurred might perhaps have made the situation appear more serious than it in reality was. He took me off in a boat lowered from an armed steamer. I had reckoned somewhat on this display of arms and had promised myself to make a profound effect on the radical elements, which must have been greatly enhanced really by the unusual time chosen for my visit to the English admiral - it was already night. I was not wrong either.

I informed the English admiral of the occurrences on board, that a Red Guard had been formed, and that a serious difference might quite conceivably arise during the night between them and the orderly portion of the crew. The officers were robbed of their weapons by the Armistice terms and so were unable to restore order by force. I therefore set myself the task of finding out what action he thought fit to take under such circumstances. I was careful to emphasise that my question was not put with the object of assuring the safety of the officers. I explained that I should be best served if the Red Guard could be removed from the ships as a German mail vessel to take them home was not in harbour at the time and would not arrive at the earliest for three days. I gave him to understand that I would like them to be interned somewhere, in the same way as on board, till this vessel sailed for home. The English admiral answered that he had no accommodation for them on land, but that he would rather take them off at once as prisoners-of-war and confine them as such on board his ships. Further, he was ready, as I was responsible for the maintenance of discipline, to support my authority with all the power at his disposal and to maintain it. I was to tell my men that he would take the most drastic steps if they went so far as to disobey me and, if necessary, would place armed guards aboard our ships. As I could not permit my men to be taken as prisoners, and above all things did not want an English guard on board as they put the German right of possession of the ships into question, I sought a way out of this suggested solution which would yet support me in case the Red Guard refused to go home in the next mail boat as I would order. The English admiral gave me this promise with the assurance that he would place as many destroyers at my disposal as I wanted. Further, during that very night torpedo craft would he in readiness to come alongside *Friedrich der Grosse* if the signals arranged between us were made.

After my return on board I was able to secure general peace and quiet. I informed the crew of the gist of the conference I had had. The next morning a meeting of the ship's company took place; the Red Guard declared itself as ready to take the next transport home; they promised not to disturb order and discipline in the meantime, but begged that they would not be put on board the steamer by an English armed guard. I promised this and informed the English admiral. The Red Guard kept their promise. When a destroyer, cleared for action, came alongside, it surprised me too. But I could do nothing to alter it. However, the Red Guard were finally put on board the transport in an unarmed boat.

The appearance of the destroyer was not without its good, however, as some of the ship's company who observed the incident expressed loathing and disgust that, due to the unbelievable conduct of a few Germans, such a measure should become necessary.

At this time the dispatch of wireless messages was forbidden us by the English, and by the removal of essential parts of the apparatus it was also sought to make this impossible. I informed the Navy Office of this, leaving it to them whether a protest should be lodged on this account. This prohibition was not entirely unfavourable to the squadron, as it held the daily and provoking press bulletin away from the men.

It is worthy of note that a period of peace now ensued for *Friedrich der Grosse* and the rest of the squadron.

The establishment of a constitutional government in February 1919 was received with gratitude by the men, which was expressed in a telegram of allegiance addressed to the Chancellor. The dispatch originated in the cruiser *Emden* and copies were distributed for signature among the crews of the ships and torpedo boats. Only very radical crews abstained from signing, including the Head Soldiers' Councillor. Much to his discomfiture, in spite of this the telegram reached the Chancellor and the press.

Immediately after the installation of the new government the Soldiers' Councils at home were removed from their position and in their place trustworthy men were installed with various powers. For the interned squadron the order of the 24th January still held good, and the Soldiers' Councils remained in power.

I had thus to concentrate on getting the permission of the government to exercise the power of command in the internal functions of the squadron, at least, within reason.

The Head Soldiers' Councillor had co-operated somewhat in the broad headings under which the actual command of the ships was exercised, as he thought it more clever in this way to attempt to hide his hate of the government, which fact we already knew. I was certain that he would try to put a spoke in my wheel if ever he got the opportunity of making my orders unworkable. It therefore appeared now all the more important to sift the Head Soldiers' Council of its more radical delegates who neither served the interests of the squadron nor were suited to the times. But their following in the squadron was still too strong for this to be achieved by new elections. The two occasions on which these delegates had interfered with my authority, in a way to which they were not entitled, did not appear to me to be suitable ground on which to pick a quarrel with them. Then came my opportunity, when two of the most radical delegates committed a breach, of not only my orders, but of the English regulations as well. I was therefore able to proceed against them with the sure knowledge of getting rid of them: not only did I have right on my side, but might as well. I dismissed them from the position of delegates to the Head Soldiers' Council and ordered them to return to Germany by the next mail boat.

According to the regulations I was not entitled to dismiss delegates from this Council. The German senior officer in foreign waters must surely have the right to throw out incompetent delegates whose conduct endangers the friendly relations with the 'host' state. I could now also get a decision on this question.

My methods aroused a storm of indignation in the squadron, except only in the torpedo craft, in two light cruisers and two battleships, which remained undisturbed. The ship's company of my flagship saw fit to refuse their duty; one or other of the soldiers' delegates proposed that I should be dismissed. Besides this, in the usual radical manner personal remarks against me were not spared. I informed the English admiral that on account of the upheaval caused by the action I had taken, I would take no further steps against the offenders.

The decisive step for the putting aside of the unsuitable delegates had now been taken; there was, therefore, no point in fostering further dissension in the squadron. With this object I assured them that I would recall my consent, for the proceedings to go any further, from the Minister of State concerned. The upheaval then subsided somewhat and the crew of my flagship resumed their duty.

The report to the Minister of Defence, who would deal with the circumstances, had to pass the censorship of the English admiral. Thus he gained an insight into the business. The Soldiers' Councils reproached me for this, but I could easily justify my action; had I evaded the censorship I would have exposed not only myself but also the two delegates to a breach of the English regulations and thus left us defenceless.

I requested a decision by wireless from the Minister of Defence and sought further to clear up the question of various squadron proceedings (weekly correspondence service home, unsuitability of dealing with such subjects by wireless), which had not been settled, including whether I had the power to dismiss delegates of the Head Soldiers' Council if they contravened English regulations.

Meanwhile the torpedo craft and the loyal ships had ranged themselves in opposition to the agitation raised against me and were gaining ground. The unfortunate part was that until the decision of the Minister of State was received, days and weeks might go by during which time the strife about my person would not abate.

Then appeared an unexpected solution. The English admiral sent me two officers one night, a few days after this occurrence, with orders to deliver up the two ringleaders at once. If, however, I had good reasons for disagreeing with this order he would not insist upon it. I had no intention of giving them up, keeping to my promise that I would hold my shield over any German whatever his offence. I gave them both the choice; either to cease any kind of action in the Head Soldiers' Council as well as the agitation against the fleet command and to leave the ship without stir by the next transport home – or to be delivered up. I gave them time to think it over and they decided on the former course. Through their promise I had a strong grip on the situation. Were they to push their agitation any further I could still deliver them up. The order of the English admiral had a further and happy result for me, in that if the Minister of Defence did not agree to my proposals to get rid of the two delegates my views would prevail just the same. I therefore conveyed to the English admiral that I bade leave to differ on the question of delivering up the offenders as he had not learned of the infringement of the English regulations through his own people but through me. I myself had only wished to make it clear that I did not countenance such infringements. On these grounds the surrender of these men was not at all wished by me. I would, however, send them back to Germany for punishment. I undertook that they would leave the ship on the very next opportunity of a passage. After about a week and the evening before the sailing of the German mail-boat to Wilhelmshaven I received the answer by wireless from the Minister of State:

'Book-number 1780. Navy Office.

'In accordance with paragraph II of the Official Gazette of the 24th January, No. 18, H.... H.... and M.... M.... are punishable for insubordination. As loyal co-operation not established, send both home first opportunity. Letter follows.'

I did not receive the expected letter until three months later. From it I learned that my power of dismissing delegates to the Head Soldiers' Council had not been approved. This decision astonished me.

On the day of departure the two refused to leave the ship in spite of their promise; they demanded a delay until the following trip home, as they said they had to arrange for their substitutes and had not yet packed their effects. I told them that the question of substitutes had nothing to do with them, that I would deal with it and that they were to embark in two hours at the latest. I had to inform the English admiral that they apparently did not want to leave the ship on account of the arrangements for the English postal service and because their passage home had been announced. This had the result of bringing an English destroyer and an armed steamer, both cleared for action, to lie off the *Friedrich der Grosse* when the time came for them to leave the ship. They now left the ship without further incident. This business, which was witnessed by a number of ships' companies, again aroused indignation. The substitution of both the delegates was therefore final and yet considered completely in accordance with the regulations by the greater proportion of the ships. The torpedo boats had made known their trust in their delegate to the Head Soldiers' Council. He and a further delegate of the Head Soldiers' Council, whom I would liked to have kept on account of their loyalty to the navy, resigned from their positions and wished to avail themselves of the transport home. A fifth delegate was already prepared to exchange for a billet in the interned squadron party at Wilhelmshaven. Thus the Head Soldiers' Council had dissolved.

As I was compelled to order the election of a new Head Soldiers' Council in accordance with the proclamation of the 24th January, and as the crews had not yet altogether become of one mind on the subject of which line to follow, I thought it necessary that in the new elections it was to be strived for that only delegates who would promise, in the interests of the State, to work for the navy and the interned squadron would be elected to the Head Soldiers' Council. Pending the holding of the new elections, which took place a few weeks later, the Soldiers' Council of my new flagship provided me with an upright and loyal petty officer for the post of Head Soldiers' Councillor. The newly elected Head Soldiers' Council turned out to be immeasurably better than its predecessor. The majority of its delegates were loyal to the navy and animated by the best spirit to do good. As the Head Soldiers' Council was really opposed to the agitation against the squadron command, it lost the following of the radical elements as soon as it ranged itself on our side, whilst it was just what the loyal-minded, who were attached to their officers, wished. The new Head Soldiers' Councillor was unable to prevail over this internal dissension as well. Two of his delegates relapsed into the bad old ways of their predecessors but aroused such a hostile feeling amongst the stokers of my new flagship that they decided to clear out voluntarily and return to Germany. The remaining delegates who were loyal to the navy withdrew from the Head Soldiers' Council of their own accord or were withdrawn, and in the last days of the interned squadron the petty officer mentioned above representing the Head Soldiers' Council acted in its stead. This development of the Head Soldiers' Council made my task of administration easier during the remaining course of the internment and was of benefit to the whole squadron; the officers of the remaining ships had also improved their status as a result of these proceedings.

CHAPTER IV

Change of flagship - second reduction of crews

The time had come, with the turning out of the Head Soldiers' Council, to change my flagship, which I had contemplated since the end of January but did not carry out at the time owing to the existing situation. It took place on 25th March. I chose the light cruiser *Emden* as it was the only ship that had offered to place itself at my disposal in that capacity. Her ship's company was able to remain loyal to the navy under the tactful and energetic leadership of their recently recalled commanding officer, Kapitänleutnant Elze. It affected me much at that time as particularly pleasant that the whole ship - from the officer to the stoker or sailor - should ask me to change my flag to her.

For outward appearances a larger ship would have been more suitable as a flagship. To the English admiral, who inquired privately why I had chosen a light cruiser rather than a large ship, I replied that as a former light-cruiser leader I felt happier in such a ship than in any other. My staff and I never regretted the decision - captain, officers, warrant officers and men made our life on board as pleasant as it was possible under the given conditions.

The change of flagship was made known to the crews by the following circular letter:

"Many rumours are current concerning the change of flagship.
To clear the situation the following is brought to your notice.
Some of the ship's company of the *Friedrich der Grosse*, for some time past, have not behaved towards me in the manner which I, at least, had to and must insist upon. I became aware of insolent action against me. To stay on board was therefore distasteful to me; all appeals in the ship were useless.
After much hesitation I left the ship on 25th March to hoist my flag in another on whose ship's company I could rely to behave loyally. A great many ships with these qualifications were available to choose from. My choice finally settled on the *Emden* for the following reasons:
The ship is in a conveniently central position for administrative purposes and for signals. The living accommodation of a light cruiser designed as a flagship appeals to me, particularly as I lived aboard such a ship for a long time as commander of the scouting forces.
There are no other reasons for the change of flagship.
It is mischievous and laughable to suggest that I have changed my flagship in order to lead the squadron in any way differing from the former system. I have more than once announced - and in particular to the Head Soldiers' Council - that I stand by the government order of the 19th January 1919. This attitude

supports without question the instructions B 1637 of 22nd February 1919 (continuation of Soldiers' Councils) as these were put into force for the squadron.

Inasmuch as I carry out these orders and their obligations under reciprocal safeguards for my remaining rights, so must all others discharge their duty and retain their rights.

This basis must above all else be the line of conduct in the pettiest work of the squadron command and the Soldiers' Council.

For the reason that the Head Soldier's Council's proceedings until now have been of an unruly character, I am not in a position to work in co-operation with a new Head Soldiers' Council which is not prepared to abide by the proclamation of the 19th January 1919.

I must therefore stipulate that for the delegates to be elected to the new Head Soldiers' Council, they must adhere to the proclamation of the government regarding the powers of command, dated 19th January 1919."

I was not much helped by only removing the two ringleaders from the Head Soldiers' Council. I still had to get rid of a great number of these disaffected people from the squadron. As they had predominated in their representation in the previous times of turmoil they had to be got rid of. We could do without a further 150 men in the squadron without impairing our readiness for sea. A scrutiny of the lists showed that we could dismiss this number on the basis of the complements up to the year 1914 inclusive. It was arranged on the strength of these figures to send home this surplus at the first opportunity.

CHAPTER V

The "scuttling" idea

In the first few days after my return to the interned squadron I had mentioned the idea of sinking the fleet to my chief of staff. As the waves of revolutionary passion were then running high we came to the conclusion to let the matter rest for the time. The interlude of peace in things political after our transfer to the *Emden* brought it again more into the foreground, and this was stimulated by the English press, in which an idea of the peace terms to be imposed on Germany had leaked out. At the end of February I had received a letter from Kommodore Heinrich, the naval delegate to the Peace Commission, which substantiated the idea that the object of the Commission was the surrender of the ships. I was positive that this energetic and able officer would do his best to defeat this object, but I had to take into consideration that his goodwill was bounded by the decisions of the government. The latter, judging by its surrender to any and every demand of the Entente, promised no good to the ships of the interned squadron.

At the beginning of March the English Admiralty took the first steps towards a further reduction of the care and maintenance parties on board our ships and torpedo boats. The reduction ordered was considerable. For instance, battleships and heavy cruisers with a complement of about 200, to be reduced to 78 so as to correspond roughly to a figure comparable with English ships of the same class when laid up out of commission. The squadron command could not agree to this reduction for reasons of safety and because reasonable living conditions had to be maintained. We requested a reduction of between 5 and 20 in accordance with the size of ship. The English Admiralty, after our counter-proposals, did not proceed with the business, but allowed the whole matter to drop.

We could not foresee what motives underlay this preliminary action by the English Admiralty. Either they wanted to reduce the crews because of the previous disorders which had occurred or they wanted to create a favourable preliminary military condition for some sort of seizure on the occasion of the signing of peace, or perhaps they wanted a harmless excuse for not dividing the ships up amongst Allied ports, as the reduction of crews would have the result of impairing the readiness for sea of the ships. The Entente press at that time were already quietly discussing the seizure of the ships when peace was signed and rather more openly debating the therefore necessary dividing up of the ships amongst the various Entente ports. Judging by the discussions in the English press we had come to the conclusion that England had very little wish to divide up our unusually high-class ship material amongst the Allies. It was also apparent to us, knowing the English character, that this distribution of ships, through which England would have to provide herself with material to oppose an opponent of equal strength in a future war at sea, was as un-English as possible. The English press recommended instead of dividing up the German ships, to sink them, and of course this would be done by England alone.

This preliminary attack on our crew-strengths made us surmise that England would never again let go of the interned ships when peace was signed. We set our minds on this solution and in quiet pondered over the necessary steps that would have to be taken. Before I, myself, could come to a definite decision on the question of the sinking, I had to await the delivery of the peace conditions to Germany, and await their reception and effect on the country. The position now arose that the idea of sinking the ships, which had untold numbers of advocates amongst the naval officers of the interned squadron, should not be allowed to leak out by any hasty sign which would attract the attention of the men and therefore of the English and thus frustrate the sinking itself. Many officers came to see me on the subject. They had to be sharply reprimanded, in spite of my inner feelings on the question. Had I given the slightest sign of approval it would have touched a train right round the squadron. The sinking would have been discussed in the ward-rooms of the fleet. The men would have got to know about it and a single traitor need only be amongst them for the English to learn of it. I was therefore naturally scarcely understood in my detached attitude - but I had to contribute my mite for the common good.

The SMS Bayern anchored at Scapa Flow. The Bayern-class of battleship was Germany's answer to the British Queen Elizabeth class. The 28,600-ton Bayern also mounted 138cm guns, equivalent to the British 15 inch, but was generally slower.

Above: The 25,880-ton SMS Kronprinz Wilhelm. A König-class battleship, she entered service as the Kronprinz in 1914 and fought at Jutland. Five months later she was damaged by a torpedo fired from the British submarine J1. She was renamed Kronprinz Wilhelm in January 1918.

The SMS Kaiser. The lead battleship of her class, Kaiser entered service in August 1912 and suffered two-hits at Jutland.

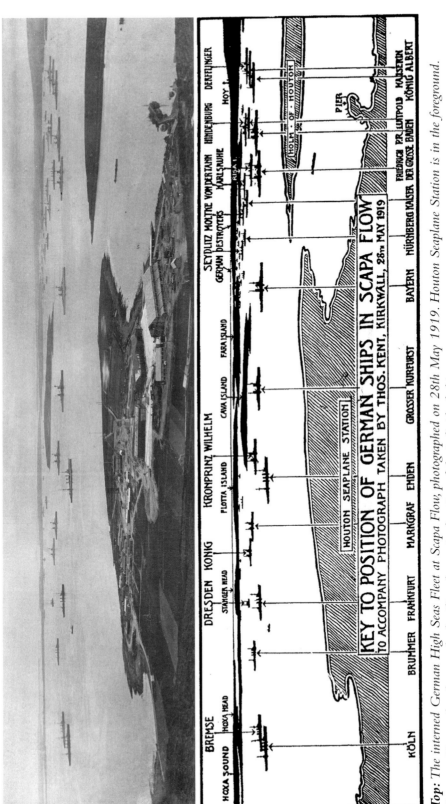

Top: The interned German High Seas Fleet at Scapa Flow, photographed on 28th May 1919. Houton Seaplane Station is in the foreground.

Bottom: Key to the photograph, detailing the precise location of the individual ships.

Above: *SMS Bayern sinking by the stern. Of the sixteen interned capital ships, Bayern was the eleventh to go down, finally sinking at 2.30 p.m.*

Opposite (viewed horizontally):

> ***Top left:*** *The capsized bow of the light cruiser Bremse. The crew of the British destroyer HMS Venetia rushed back from the torpedo practice, succeeded in boarding the Bremse and taking her in tow, but the German vessel capsized at 2.30 p.m. when only yards from being beached on the island of Cava.*
>
> ***Top right:*** *SMS Bayern, sinking by the stern.*
>
> ***Bottom left:*** *Scapa Bay, photographed from Houton at 3.00 p.m. on 21st June 1919.*
>
> ***Bottom right:*** *Scapa Bay, photographed from Houton at 3.45 p.m. on 21st June 1919.*

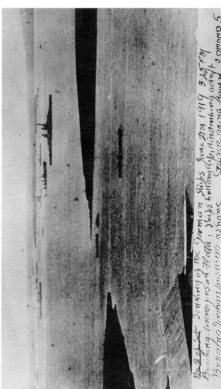

No.2 of Set. Drawing of the German Ships June 21st 1919 3.45 PM
Beaching (coming) rest of Flotta. Ships bottom-up, Hindenburg adrift
B7445745 German prisoners as hore
SEIDLITZ 90 MG Anna at S.OMOND 5

No.1 OS. Set. The sinking of the German Ships June 21st 1919. 3PM
a lying course torpedo boats, Two Ships bottom up Cruiser sinking (the
FOR the D. no B   Baden ashore

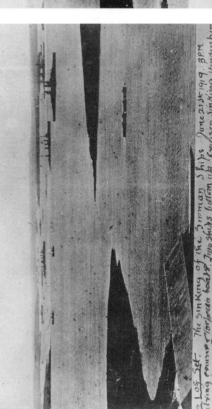

Four stages in the sinking of the German Battleship Markaraf in Scapa Flow on June 21st 1919.

J. Omond M.L.

The SMS Markgraf was the last battleship to sink at 4.45 p.m. on 21st June 1919.

Von Reuter's old ship, the 26,600-ton battlecruiser Derfflinger, photographed four minutes before sinking at 2.45 p.m. on 21st June 1919.

Above: *An armed British boarding party prepares to board one of the German torpedo boats in Gutter Sound.*

Below: *The torpedo boats V83 and G92 of the 14th Half Flotilla, beached on the east coast of Risa.*

CHAPTER VI

Influence of the internment on the ships' companies

Our duty was really not uninteresting and never without tension, but it was hardly ever elevating; the joys that life has to give and which warmed and lightened our existence from outside were thirstily accepted.

The absolute isolation from the land certainly had an unhappy effect on the minds of the ships' companies in spite of all efforts to find suitable diversions. The life aboard the big ships was, however, always more endurable than that in the torpedo boats. Aboard the former there was at least room for lectures, for spiritual and professional welfare, for exercise and sport of all kinds, and the majority of the crews had always one volunteer or another with the talent to entertain and refresh the mind. The torpedo boats were living in quite different circumstances; here arose the peculiar discomfort from the fact that the slightest seaway rolled each pair of boats, which lay lashed together, against each other, and the heavy thuds, as well as the ensuring of the safety of the boats, kept the crews awake on most nights. Nevertheless these very ships' companies, from officer to man, met all these efforts and privations in a spirit which has been too little known; they always appeared to be sprightly, cheerful, and full of good spirits, with the shining example before them all of their leader, Korvettenkapitän Cordes. The number of senior officers and petty officers should also be noted particularly, who put up with this confinement in a very limited space and in spite of this carried out their duty with all their old loyalty. In particular do I think of Marine Oberstabs-Ing. Faustmann in this connection, who in the double duty of Squadron Engineer Officer and chief engineer of the *Markgraf* was always at his post. Nothing was able to destroy his sense of humour and cheerfulness in his duty. He served the squadron well, and finally, after his worthy captain was killed, he brought the sinking of the *Markgraf* to a successful conclusion. The monotony of the internment did not affect the keenness or attention to duty of the senior members of my staff either: Marine-Stabsarzt Doctor Lange, Marine-Kriegsgerichtsrat Loesch, and Stabs-Zahlmeister Habicht. Their sound way of thinking and their personal character, varied though these were, stimulated me and brought me into close personal touch with them.

The efforts to get films sent out for diversion and entertainment were for a long time unsuccessful, and the first few only began to arrive just before the sinking. They were received with rapture. Dental problems worked their depressing influence far and wide; in spite of urgent representations the Navy Office was unable to provide a dentist until the fleet was already sinking. To be welcomed was the fact that the spiritual needs of the navy were looked after by Chaplain Ronneberger, the protestant, and Chaplain Esterkand, the catholic minister, who were both equal to their task and did much to lift the general tone of the fleet.

All ranks and ratings, officers, sailors, and stokers, were filled with anxiety for the future due to the gloomy and confused conditions in the State, which appeared to have a tendency to drag us still lower. The news from home gave one the not quite unjustifiable feeling that those who were away from home would not be sufficiently regarded in the re-modelling of the navy. Because of this general attitude, the head of the Admiralty, whose good intentions were without question - gave them expression by sending an officer to the interned squadron to make a note of our wishes - could not do enough for the interned ranks and ratings to allay their anxiety.

The internment weighed so heavily on the men that they reached a state in which the slightest incident would have driven them to disorders and disturbances. The political agitators seized on these incidents; they nursed these grievances so that the squadron had no peace until the last big reduction just before the sinking and our right of possession of the ships was endangered during all this time. I will only mention two especially grave incidents out of the total. In the one case a number of men had gathered during the night in a previously well-behaved battleship and hoisted the red flag at the jackstaff with a great deal of noise. Then, as an English patrol vessel approached, attracted by the commotion, it was hauled down again. The ship's company, indignant at this occurrence, demanded the severe punishment of the ringleaders. As the carrying out of cell punishment in the squadron (as was the case, too, at home) did not seem sufficiently certain, they underwent their punishment in an English prison at Perth and were thereafter sent back to Germany, as this kind of imprisonment, coupled with a journey through the Scottish Highlands, was a pleasant break in the internment and might encourage further disorders. The second case occurred on board another battleship and dragged on from the end of April to the middle of May. It finally culminated in serious disorders; these, deservedly, could be met by cell punishment, but this was opposed by the crew, who were led by communist agitators. The instigators were soon unmasked and at my request were kept in custody awaiting court martial on board an English battleship until the next mail-boat left for Wilhelmshaven. This disorder was the reason for the last big reduction of the crews.

The impulse to escape from the internment had become so strong that many men created trouble with the sole idea that, in accordance with court-martial procedure, as a verdict could not be given at Scapa Flow they would be sent back to the Homeland. This way out of the internment seemed all the less difficult for them, as it was the talk of the squadron that those awaiting inquiry by court martial on their return home were at once given long leave and that the court martial might subsequently not take place at all.

As on board most ships it was impossible to carry out cell punishment, and as money fines could unfortunately not be inflicted, there was nothing else left to do in the squadron, if its seaworthiness was to be maintained, except to overlook the transgressions rather than send the men home; in this way a great number of men escaped their well-deserved punishment. To have attempted to exchange the interned crews for fresh personnel from Germany was out of the question, as the experiences we had had with the personnel already sent back to Scapa Flow had been very troublesome in a political sense.

They forced me to isolate Scapa Flow, apart from the officers, as regards reliefs.

The internment weighed on us all. Still, what comradely friendship could not give us, and what the hate of the enemy could not rob us of, was the wonder of nature at Scapa Flow.

The scenery around us was really harsh, and desolate. Water, mountains, otherwise nothing. And yet this forgotten corner of the Earth had its attractions, its beauty - not by day, during glaring sunlight or when the rain-clouds painted everything grey on grey, but in the evening or by night. Then it was that the Northern Lights would cast their rays like searchlights over the clouds and light them to a yellow hue, then again pour themselves over the whole firmament in a single sea of fire. And the sunsets, wonderful in their coloured splendour! It was during a May evening, the sun sank to the horizon at a late hour and all the colours of which it seemed possessed was poured over the evening sky; the spectacle was overpowering and enchanting. And then, as though this were not of sufficient splendour, the Northern Lights flung their fiery streams into the blaze - the clouds were fired and in their flaming fire rose the dark, naked cliffs of the mountains of Orkney. There is yet a God!

CHAPTER VII

Preparations for the scuttling – last reduction of the crews

On 11th May the peace terms imposed by the Entente became known in the interned squadron through the reports in the newspapers. For a day or two it lay like lead on the minds of the men. Then, however, their German unconcern and indifference, countering the anxiety for the welfare of their own country, won the upper hand, and the hope that the internment would now soon be over helped further to draw attention away from the extraordinarily severe conditions of the peace terms. The time had now come when I had to study the possible consequences of the refusal or acceptance of the peace terms by the German Government and appreciate the situation, in order to reach conclusions that would guide my actions.

That I should be left entirely to my own devices was quite clear to me. I had refused orders and instructions, as I alone and no one at home could judge and appreciate the situation in the interned squadron.

There were three possible ways in which the peace terms might be treated: the German Government might refuse the conditions; they might negotiate, which was the most probable; or they could at once accept the conditions, which seemed unlikely by the very severity of the terms.

(a) Refusal

In this case the renewal of hostilities had to be reckoned on. That England would permit the German ships, which in spite of internment in England had remained in German hands, to journey back to Germany would not have seemed possible even to the most rabid German pacifist or socialist. It was much more likely that England would not only take possession of our excellent ships but rather that she would take this step against us with a particular and malicious joy and with great enthusiasm. To allow England to take possession of the German fleet would therefore be treason. The unreadiness for action of the ships and their defenceless state would have made this treachery appear even worse. For us officers it was unthinkable to surrender defenceless ships to the enemy. As, at the beginning of the war, this had been again emphasised by a decision of the All Highest, this could well be taken as sufficient support for the action of the officers. At the threat of danger of war or the renewal of hostilities we officers were bound by this decision of the All Highest to destroy the German ships, to sink them. It had not been repealed by the new government. Our right and our duty to sink the ships was beyond question. As the ships had remained in the possession of the German Government, we alone were responsible for what we did with them and should never be answerable to the Entente! If the Allied port were damaged by the sinking, the Entente itself would be to blame as they had cheated us in the carrying out of the Armistice arrangements by which the German ships were to have been laid up in neutral harbours.

Two obstacles thereupon arose in the carrying out of the sinking: the restriction of our postal service with the German Admiralty and the state of mind of the crews of the interned ships.

From the 8th May onwards, that is from the date the peace conditions were made known to Germany, the strictest censorship was imposed on the interned squadron. The date of the re-imposition of these restrictions shows beyond question that they were intended to keep us in the dark regarding the peace negotiations and particularly as regarded the threat of war or renewal of hostilities by cutting us off from communication with the Homeland. The new censorship regulations, amongst other things, laid down that the outgoing mail from Germany, which until then had gone straight from the mail-boat uncensored to the ships, had now to go through the English censors in London. This deviation of the mail meant a delay of from three to four weeks! The protests made against this were not considered; the British Government considered it 'essential' that the censorship should be carried out only in London. The delay in the mails, as was emphasised in the protest, could only worsen the state of mind of the crews, which was already bad enough owing to the long internment. Perhaps this was a further cunning move on the part of the English to break the spirit of the crews and thereby to bring pressure on the German Government to reduce the numbers of the men. Then when the Entente had made the stealing or taking over of the ships all the easier, or by emphasising the hardships had convinced the German Government, the government might soon be glad to get rid of this unhappy squadron. In any case the tightening of the censorship seemed such an extraordinary measure to me that it impressed me with the idea of keeping the sharpest watch where England was concerned.

It became apparent that the English Admiralty was doing all it could, at the very moment when matters were coming to a head and the danger of hostilities being resumed was imminent, to prevent any further news from reaching me from Germany. I had therefore to reckon on the fact that the English admiral might try to surprise me at any moment, seize the ships, and confiscate them. It goes without saying that no steps would be too drastic, whatever the consequences, to make certain of sinking the ships, even though it had to be delayed till the last minute. I put my trust in my captains, so that even though the enemy tried to take us by surprise we should remain masters of the situation.

The second obstacle: the state of mind of the ships' companies made it seem improbable that they would be won over to co-operate without exception in the sinking, under the very muzzles of the English guns. Certain preliminary steps to prepare for the sinking were unavoidable, and it was to be feared that someone or other would give away our intended operation to the English admiral. But even if the preparations could be got through without the knowledge of the men, they might still try and prevent it or even counter it under the influence of the English gunfire on the actual day. The officers, in such a case, would not have been able to carry through their intentions due to their loss of authority and because they had been deprived of their arms.

This obstacle could only be disposed of by reducing the strength of the crews. At that time the reduction of the men could not even be considered as it might have been a stab in the back for the German Government which might then be engaged in the negotiations for the return of the ships. The reduction would have been construed in English circles as showing that the idea of returning the ships, which until then had been kept in a state of readiness for sea, had been given up by the squadron. Had we, the internees, ourselves given up the idea of the homeward journey of the ships it would have suited the machinations of the Entente most admirably – in fact our attitude would clinch the belief that the government was behind us and that its official views should not be taken too seriously. Out of these considerations I decided to issue no orders on the subject for the present. Of course, I ran the risk that the government might curtly decline the proposed peace terms, though this was indeed no great risk; judging by their mentality they were far more likely to choose the way of negotiation. I could still wait and see; it seemed to me wiser than reducing it all to a gamble by trying to force the play.

(b) What should the interned squadron expect to be the
outcome of the negotiations over the peace terms?

It was possible that the German Government might use the ships as an asset in bartering, e.g. in exchange for a free hand in the Baltic or to ensure the emancipation of the Saar district[11]. In such a case the German fleet would have fulfilled an object and could have been handed over to the enemy. This solution would, of course, have been an unpleasant one for us officers, but for the future and welfare of the State we should have brought ourselves to this sacrifice. Whether the government intended to pursue such a course was, for me, the one and only question that gave me no peace until the actual day of the sinking. All my verbal inquiries for information remained unanswered. That the fleet might be offered for sale did, of course, not come into our deliberations; we could not believe such a solution by the government could be proposed. It was possible, of course, that the government was already pledged to sell the ships and that they kept us officers, indispensable to them for the moment, in the dark about their intentions as they knew, quite rightly, that we would not lend a hand to such an undertaking and would sooner refuse duty.

Further, it was possible that the German Government was not greatly concerned over the surrender of the ships and attached no great importance to it. Honour and the rights and responsibilities of the nation meant nothing to them. This being so, it was hopeless to think that the fleet would ever return.

Our naval representative could not very well do much to alter this. Army and navy interests were opposed to each other and at the head of the Peace Commission was the Minister of the Foreign Office. The latter had always handed a portion of the blame for any mistakes he made on to the fleet. We could therefore be certain that the president of the Commission in particular would put in no word for the maintenance of the German fleet if its importance were weighed against that of the army. On the contrary, the German fleet would be sacrificed without a second thought in the same way that the U-boat war was treated.

As in the question of the considerations up to paragraph B it seemed wisest for the moment to wait and see how things would shape.

(c) The effect of the immediate acceptance of the peace terms

did not need to be considered, as by all reports of happenings in the homeland published in the English press, this was the last course which was to be expected. However, the squadron command was bound, also in the event of a later acceptance of the terms, not to fulfil any conditions, particularly the surrender of the fleet without the express order of the German Government. There could be no question of the English taking possession of the ships purely on the grounds of the peace treaty being signed, as, by my isolation from the German Government, I had always to consider the possibility of the ships being bartered. Any attempt to take possession of the ships without my express consent would have had the immediate consequence of the ships being sunk.

At the end of April the serious disorders already mentioned broke out on board a battleship.

This occurrence and one or two incidents of a less grave character on board other ships might have been the result of the long internment and proved the need for a change. A circular letter, originated in another battleship, addressed to all ships' companies, which came to our knowledge at the end of May, confirmed this supposition. In it, it was suggested that to shorten the internment it was no use arranging for isolated ships to refuse duty, the men should go on strike together; that would have a profound effect on the German Government to secure their release.

Such a 'General Strike' at this time, when the whole destiny of the interned squadron had reached its last crisis, might yet in the end bring about the seizure of the ships by the English. In face of this danger all misgivings about the reduction of the number of men, which had held sway until then, had to be cast aside and the lesser evil accepted. My chief of staff therefore suggested that I should send all those who were weary of the internment back to Germany. As I myself had almost reached the same conclusion, and as it would work in with the important scheme for the sinking of the ships, I gave my approval to the suggestion. The reduction would be carried out with enough severity to ensure that the sinking would be completed with certainty. The state of readiness for sea was thereby dropped.

The numbers of the crew were to be reduced as follows for heavy cruisers by 75 hands, battleships by 50, light cruisers by 20; the leader of the torpedo boats would fix the numbers by which the torpedo boats' crews were to be reduced.

We were supported in our reduction of the numbers of the men by the fact that the nights had become as bright as day, which made artificial lighting in the spaces that were lit naturally unnecessary. The few remaining men could be accommodated in these spaces. Further, as the English were supplying the drinking and boiler water it was no longer necessary to keep steam in a boiler. The steam galleys could be supplied by the steam pinnaces. Coal and provisions were to be had in profusion, care and maintenance work no longer had to be reckoned on. It was therefore only necessary to keep as many men aboard as were required for cooking, and for letting go or weighing the sheet anchor.

The following proposals for reduction were sent to the German Admiralty – the English admiral was informed officially through the usual channels:

WIRELESS MESSAGE ADDRESSED TO THE ADMIRALTY, BERLIN

'It is now of the utmost importance to relieve the interned crews without delay, at the latest the first batch of 2,700 men must be sent home at the beginning of June. As a preliminary measure reliefs will not be insisted on. The personnel remaining on board will suffice for the maintenance of the safety of the ships, and will be sufficient to ensure that the right of possession to the interned ships and torpedo boats of the German Government is not impaired. The readiness for sea of the material will be maintained as far as possible with the means at our disposal. Reliefs for the personnel remaining behind must be arranged at once so that they, too, can be sent home with little delay after the first batch. A reply by return, by wireless, that the return home of the men is approved is absolutely necessary.'

The German Admiralty willingly consented to our proposal, as did the English, and after a few days I received the official permission to proceed with the reduction. The English Admiralty were, of course, only too pleased, as it fitted in most opportunely with their previously formulated designs for seizing the ships. The German Admiralty made preparations for the selection of transport vessels. These kept us waiting longer than we cared for, but taking the upheavals in Germany into consideration it was impossible to expect them at Scapa Flow earlier than between the 15th and 17th of June.

The disorders previously mentioned, then, supplied the basis out of which grew the practical possibility of effecting the sinking which was to save us from dishonour and shame.

The order for the reduction was received with approval in the squadron. Only one of the ships' companies, that of a heavy cruiser, gave rein to their indignation, as expressed in a letter they circulated amongst the other ships, and this indignation was because they said the admiral had dared to give an 'order' to four thousand men! Eventually they too preferred to conform to my orders and not give up the journey home.

The proposed numbers of men to be dispensed with were not quite reached, as I did not then want to instruct the various commanders as to my final intention – the sinking. The counter-proposals of the various commanders, with few exceptions, did not greatly exceed the numbers to be retained that I had in view. The conclusions the various commanders of ships reached, in regard to the number of men to be kept to ensure satisfactory living conditions, naturally varied. Where the figures appeared to be much too high they were brought down to a more reasonable number.

The 31st May, and with it the festival of the victory at the Battle of Skagerrak, approached. Rumours reached us in the squadron command that the English were contemplating seizing the ships at about this time, and from the English drifters' crews we learnt that preparations were going forward on board the English ships for the accommodation of the German crews. The squadron command could attach no credence to these reports, the ships being seized purely because it was the 1st June was not possible. Still the attitude of the German crews on this day might perhaps furnish them with an excuse, and in the strained atmosphere of the times might lead on to the seizure and confiscation of the ships. For this reason the commanding officers were ordered to be prepared to sink their ships if the enemy attempted to seize them, and by keeping a careful watch to avoid being surprised; on no account were the men to gain an inkling of the steps being taken. For the men an open order was issued to the squadron that they might worthily celebrate the occasion down below, but were to avoid all open display, which would show from outboard. This appeal to the men was not heeded. They were not to be persuaded from this on the 31st May of all days and made the celebration as open as possible with flags and illuminations, that is both by day and night. The day passed, in spite of numerous interferences by the English guard boats, without the German ships being seized.

At the beginning of June I learned that the crews of the torpedo boats were making preparations for the sinking of their boats. These preparations, had they become known in the squadron, might have made the sinking of the fleet impossible. I sent for the leader of the torpedo boats to come aboard the *Emden* and told him of my appreciation of the situation and of my intentions. He announced his agreement. He succeeded in keeping his preparations secret, not only from the English, but also from the rest of the squadron; not an easy thing to do by any means.

Weeks of extreme tension followed. We were entirely dependent on the English press for information as to the progress and substance of the peace negotiations as our mails, both letters and papers, had to pass the English censorship in London and only reached us after a delay of from three to four weeks. Even the English newspapers, at the best, were four days old and their assertions were contradictory, sensationally coloured, unreliable, and filled with hate. It was difficult to appreciate the state of the negotiations and particularly to gather what attitude the German Government and people had taken up. The German mail and provision vessels, although always begged to bring over newspapers, usually only had a copy of the paper issued on the day they sailed. I received nothing from the Admiralty; of course, they themselves were not in the picture and had no information to give. At last I did at least receive a much-asked-for German copy of the peace conditions. In this I saw that at the conclusion of peace the German ships were to be surrendered to the Allied powers. It was not clear whether the ships were to be handed over at the conclusion of the preliminary negotiations or whether this was to be done after peace had been officially ratified. I therefore adopted the same attitude both for myself and on behalf of the interned squadron that the Entente would in its execution of official peace, that is, in the ratification by the three States, i.e. I would not have admitted the right of the English Government to seize the ships at the conclusion of the preliminary acceptance of peace unless, of course, the German Government had previously furnished me with orders to the contrary. Such an attempt on the part of the Entente I would have regarded as an act of violence and would have answered it by sinking the ships. Up to the very day of the sinking of the fleet the German Government gave me no direction as to whether the preliminary peace or the ratified peace was to be taken as the decisive occasion. Perhaps the mail-boat which arrived at Scapa Flow after the sinking had such a letter for me; possibly the letter is still detained by the censor in London? Judging by the conversations between our men and the crews of the drifters I was certain that the English admiral would take possession of the German ships on the day the preliminary peace was signed. The correctness of my judgment was inadvertently proved by the English admiral himself, in his speech condemning the sinking given on the 22nd June. In it he mentioned the letters that were just being completed to inform us of the conclusion of peace. One letter would have sufficed for this. By the very numbers of the letters it undoubtedly proved that they were to be directed to all the ships and were to make the seizure of the ships quite plain.

In case I were prevented, on the day of the signing of peace, from giving the order to sink the ships myself, the later order for sinking the ships was added to paragraph 6 as a concluding sentence; this made certain that they would be sunk in spite of hindrances. This concluding sentence runs as follows:

'A demand for the surrender of any ship by the English, unless with my express approval, is to be regarded as a forcible attempt at seizure, and is therefore to be answered by the scuttling of the ship.'

The speech of the Minister of State, Scheidemann[12], in the Reichstag, on the subject of the peace treaty, with the slogan of 'the withered hand,' had gradually filtered through to us, and according to that it seemed likely that we would have to reckon on the refusal of the German Government to accept the terms. The little we were able to glean from the knowledge of the officers in the mail boat made it also appear not improbable that hostilities would be resumed if our counter-proposals were not accepted. The squadron command, in accordance with this appreciation of the situation, committed their intention to paper in the orders for the scuttling. The orders were to be sent to the leader of the torpedo boats and to the commanding officers of the ships as soon as the reduction of the crews had been effected. The tension grew the longer the transport steamers were delayed. The peace negotiations seemed to be getting perilously close to their conclusion; we were full of anxiety in case the transports should not arrive in time, as on this depended the reduction and on that the successful carrying out of the sinking! At last, on the 15th June, the first transport appeared and on the 17th the second. The men were quickly sent on board and the ships sailed. On 17th June, as soon as the transports had sailed, the orders were brought into force. The distribution of the orders was only partly carried out by my barge, as I thought a general distribution might awake the interest of the enemy. I therefore ordered the letters to be sent round by the English dispatch boat. The order read as follows:

Interned Squadron Command   17 June 1919.

Reference Number P. 39.
To pass through the hands of Officers only!
PERSONAL!

TO ALL COMMANDING OFFICERS AND THE LEADER OF THE TORPEDO BOATS

1. The necessary preparations are to be made at once to ensure that the ship can be sunk as quickly as possible on the receipt of an order.

2. Complete preparations are to be made as soon as the surplus men are disembarked. It is left to individual commanders to decide how far individual men are to be called in to help, and how much they should be allowed to know of my intention without in any way imperilling the scheme, e.g. by treason to the English.

3. The following preliminary steps are to be taken; all doors down below and scuttles are to be left open, such as bulkhead doors, bunker doors, all doors in longitudinal and athwartships bulkheads, gangway hatches, ventilators, square ports, etc. Depending on the opinion of the commanding officers the following further steps may be taken: the necessary measures for the rapid opening of the torpedo-tubes, the opening of a condenser, the opening of valves and sluices, to the sea with the exception of the last, etc.

4. Boats. If possible not more than one boat - for rescuing the crew - is to be cleared away ready for lowering. A flag of truce is to be prepared to take away in the boat. The boats with the crews on board are to make for the nearest land; they will remain together

under the orders of their officers.

5. The scuttling will take place:
   (a) In the case of unprovoked seizure by the English.
   (b) On the receipt of an order to that effect from me.

6. Add to 5 (a). Commanding officers are carefully to consider the necessary steps to be taken to ensure that the ships are sunk for certain, in case the English should attempt to take the ships by surprise. A demand for the surrender of any ship by the English, unless with my express approval, is to be regarded as a forcible attempt at seizure, and is therefore to be answered by the sinking of the ship.

7. Add to 5 (b). Orders may be given either (a) to sink the ship at once, or (b) to sink the ship at a certain definite time.

8. Signals. For immediate sinking as in 7 (a), the following signal will be made:
   "To all commanding officers and the torpedo boat leader. Paragraph 11. Acknowledge. Chief of the Interned Squadron."
   This signal is to be passed on by every means possible. The sinking of the ships is then to be begun at once.
   For sinking the ships at a certain definite time as in 7 (b), the following signal will be made:
   "To all commanding officers and the torpedo boat leader. Paragraph 0, 9, 1, 3. Acknowledge. Chief of the Interned Squadron."
   In this signal the first two figures refer to the date, i.e. the 9th and the two last figures to the hour, at which the sinking is to commence. The time will be reckoned from noon to noon (astronomical).

9. Acknowledgment. The receipt of the signal is to be acknowledged as follows:
   "To the Chief of the Interned Squadron. Paragraph .... is acknowledged." C.O., *Emden*."

10. As the negotiations for the acceptance or non-acceptance of the peace terms have now reached their crisis, and the resumption of hostilities may be imminent the next few days are particularly critical. From Wednesday the 18th June onwards, increased watchfulness by day and night will be necessary, not only for any suspicious move on the part of the English, but also for signals from the *Emden*. As absolute reliance cannot be placed on the men, the officers themselves must take over the necessary lookout duties.

11. It is my intention to sink the ships only if the enemy attempts to seize them without the consent of our government. Should our government agree to the peace conditions in which the ships are to be surrendered, the ships will then be handed over, to the lasting

shame of those who put us in this position.

12. Commanding officers are to keep this document locked up; it must not fall into the hands of the enemy.

(Signed) von Reuter

The secrecy of my intention to carry out the sinking was kept in all but two ships.

During the morning of 20th June I received a report from the commanding officer of a heavy cruiser that his ship's company was following his preparations for sinking the ship with mistrust and dogging his footsteps wherever he went in the ship. He therefore requested permission to acquaint his men with the orders for the sinking so that he might complete the preparations. My chief of staff recommended the approval of the request, though I thought myself that it would be better to let this heavy cruiser drop out of the scheme rather than jeopardise the whole secret. On top of this the commanding officer of a battleship informed me that four petty officers in his ship had guessed my intention by the preparations which had been made, that they wished to have nothing to do with it and had requested to be sent home at once; if their request were granted they would not give away the preparations for the sinking. Regarding secrets between Germans a variation of Goethe's saying can be quoted: 'And holds he but a tenth he holds the town entire.' If the men did not receive the news about the sinking officially, but through these petty officers, that is by way of the back stairs, they would naturally be mistrustful, reluctant and spoil the scheme. The men had now to be informed of the sinking for the very reason of avoiding treachery.

The order, which was soon passed to the men, changed their outlook considerably and restored their spirits, and the new order was circulated that afternoon to the ships and torpedo boats by the English dispatch boat.

The composition and the making of copies of this second order for the sinking had occupied the squadron command well into the afternoon, so that it was not until the evening that I could attend to the news in the English papers. *The Times* of 16th June 1919 had the following item:

OFFICIAL SUMMARY

'Under the proviso of a financial arrangement, Germany is prepared to surrender not only the surface warships demanded, but all ships of the line.'

Judging from this it was apparent that the German Government, on the supposition of a sale, was prepared to surrender not only the surface warships demanded, but all ships of the line as well, and in this included the ships of the interned squadron. The German navy in this way was being humiliated for a second time in its short history by being again offered for sale.

What wounded me most was that we had been led to believe, in the months gone by, that the government would insist on the ships returning home; instead of this they had immediately offered to surrender more ships than the Entente had demanded!

I did not want to soil my hands in this dirty business and found that my officers and officials shared my views - let the government send out their own agents whose sense of honour was perhaps less sensitive. I originated a wireless message to the German Government, saying that we officers and higher officials protested against the sale of the fleet, that we would have no hand in it, and demanded that before the sale we should be recalled and sent back home.

The above wireless message would not reach the English admiral, in accordance with the English regulations, before the next morning, Saturday the 21st June, between 8 and 9 o'clock, and that, by the first English dispatch boat. The English ships had already weighed anchor when my message was sent to the admiral, and were on their way out of harbour. He had been asked to transmit it with as little delay as possible. I do not think it was ever passed on to the German Government; the events of the day probably prevented it.

The same copy of *The Times*, referred to above, gave us the further news, on page II, that the German Government would receive a respite of five days after the answers to the German counter-proposals had been received, during which the peace treaty was to be signed or its terms refused. The three days settled for the Armistice were to be included in the period of respite. As it also appeared from the English press that England had given her answer to our counter-proposals on Monday 16th June, it was to be assumed that the Armistice would automatically cease without further warning on the Saturday. I pondered over it and assumed that the Armistice would expire at noon on Saturday, as it was natural that an Armistice should come to an end at midday to allow for the necessary advance of troops to be made by daylight.

CHAPTER VIII

The scuttling

Midsummer's Day - sunshine and calm heralded a wonderfully warm and still summer's day.

At about 10 o'clock in the morning Fregattenkapitän Oldekop informed me that the English admiral, with battleships and destroyers, had left harbour for the open sea; that the noisy English press advocated the refusal of the Entente to buy the German ships, demanding their unconditional surrender instead, and that the German postal torpedo boat was due at Scapa Flow the next day at noon. I gave the order to make the prearranged signal for 'Ships to be sunk at once.'

As, at this time, owing to the reduced personnel, signals were only exchanged between certain hours and communication had to be re-established, a certain time elapsed before the signal had been passed round the fleet and was acknowledged by the ships and the leader of the torpedo boats. At about half-past eleven the acknowledgments began to arrive.

I held back the order to sink my flagship, *Emden*, for the moment. Two English dispatch boats lay alongside, as usual, and besides them a water-boat, which had started to pump its supply of water into the *Emden*'s tanks. The crews of these boats could not have failed to notice the suppressed excitement of the *Emden*'s ship's company had I given the order at once. They would have made a noise, attracted the English admiral back, and have prevented the sinking of the remaining ships.

Shortly after 12 o'clock the *Friedrich der Grosse* took up more and more of a list whilst steadily sinking deeper, her boats were already lowered and lay off aft - now the loud and vigorous tones of single strokes of the ship's bell sounded across the water, the signal for 'Abandon ship!' We saw the crew man the boats and shove off. *Friedrich der Grosse* heeled more over on her side, torrents of water poured into her through her opened ports - then, in a few minutes, she capsizes and sinks into the depths, the air expelled through the funnels throwing up two spouts of water - then all is quiet, small fragments of wreckage float in the empty berth. The time is sixteen minutes past twelve.

The signal by the bell appeared to wake up all the remaining ships at one stroke - as though they had just been awaiting this sign - increased activity was evident on all sides, here boats were being lowered, there men could be seen hauling their heavy bags of clothes on to the quarter-decks. Again, as elsewhere, boats were being manned and shoved off from their ships with farewell cheers. There was, besides, an English guard boat, which for some time had been lying near the *Friedrich der Grosse*, whose anxiety must have been aroused by the bell signal and the simultaneous manning of the boats. Indeed, it must have observed the unusually heavy list of the ships with attention and anxiety. It became so panic-stricken when suddenly the gigantic vessel close before its eyes capsized and sank, that with never a thought it opened a wild fire on the unarmed, weaponless occupants of the boats, despite the fact that these held up white flags. At the same time it set its steam siren in action - its anxious-sounding tone startled the crews of the remaining English guard boats out of their daydreams, which on a warm summer's morning and in the absence of the admiral were only too understandable, and, as was to be expected, the sudden change from idyllic peace to the utmost tumult had the usual effect on untutored minds. They lost their heads and raged blindly against everything that did not appear to them to follow the usual routine. A panic had broken out amongst them, into which the destroyers that had remained in harbour also joined. Under the influence of this panic, acts of ferocity were committed against the unarmed German crews, which remove any English right to be indignant over German violators of the rules of war. A fortunate point was that as the consummation of the sinking proceeded *König Albert*, *Moltke*, *Brummer* quickly followed *Friedrich der Grosse*, others were on the point of sinking - the number of boats with shipwrecked crews grew to such an extent that the English boats in their perplexity often appeared not to know which boat they were to shoot at first. For this reason they quickly changed from one boat to another; due to this incessant change of target their fire did not have very grave consequences.

The sinking of the *Friedrich der Grosse*, and of the *Brummer*, which lay close astern of the *Emden*, had also aroused the English boats lying alongside us. The *Emden's* ship's company themselves, as they were down below at lunch, did not yet know of what was going on in the harbour. Now, however, it was also time to give the order to sink the *Emden*. Under the direction of the commanding officer the valves and underwater broadside torpedo tubes were opened; the water poured in. One of the English dispatch boats wanted to shove off, as they were afraid of being drawn down into the depths with the *Emden*; I kept it fast just long enough to embark the *Emden's* crew.

As the English fire on the German boats did not cease, in spite of the white flags displayed, I decided to go ashore and see the admiral commanding to get him to stop the firing. Unacquainted with the whereabouts of this admiral's office and not knowing the landing place, I transferred, with my staff, to the other English dispatch boat, which was the one kept ready for me for my visits of inspection. It landed us in a rocky bay. Already from a distance I had noticed a motorcar approaching the spot at full speed. In it sat a young gentleman dressed in tennis clothes. The coxswain of the drifter indicated him as commanding on land. To me he seemed much too young. I requested him to have the firing stopped at once. He was exceedingly angry, hardly listened, and really didn't understand a word I had to say; he ran away, returned shortly afterwards with a camera, threw himself into a speed-boat lying ready for him and drove out of the bay. I took it that he would stop the shooting. But there I was wrong. The English drifter was to take us back to the *Emden*. Whilst leaving the bay - the tide was still on the ebb - we ran hard and fast on a shoal. All efforts, that is on our own initiative, failed to float the clumsy and heavily built boat. The hillocks round the bay hid our ships, only my admiral's flag, hoisted in the *Emden*, showed above the chain of hills - it would not, would not disappear! We had to sit on that shoal, cut off from all happenings in the world, for about an hour; at last, with the setting in of the flood we floated and could steer out of the bay.

What a sight! In front of us the *Grosser Kurfürst* reared herself steeply into the air. Both cables parted with a loud clinking; she fell heavily to port and capsized. The red coating of her bottom shone wide over the blue sea.

Many berths were already 'vacated' for the journey to the bottom.

English destroyers with foam at the bows steered into the bight. One of them goes alongside *Emden* and makes efforts to slip the cable so as to tow her into shallow water. The *Emden* sinks first a little deeper. I gave up heading for the *Emden* and ordered the drifter to close on the *Bayern*, whose men lying and sitting on life-saving rafts, were floating about near their ship. We took them on board. Immediately after this the *Bayern* heeled over and the water poured below in torrents through the scuttles and ports, which, here again, were wide open. In a few minutes the quarterdeck was awash. The mighty ship then turned over and sank to the bottom with the German flag flying. Three cheers from her crew give her the tribute of honour on her last journey. The feeble wind now bears over to us the sound of the salvoes fired by the English destroyers, which are trying to prevent our work of destruction amongst the torpedo boats. A hard and hot engagement is being fought over there. Once again the cheerful battle-spirit of these wonderful officers and men is aroused - this time weapons are of no use to them; they have none, except their sense of duty. On the strength of this alone they carry out their work of destruction in the face of the heavy fire of the enemy destroyers and guard boats. The Sixth Flotilla had an especially difficult task. They did not get the signal, through untoward circumstances, until much later on, at a time when the English, who had at first lost their heads, were beginning to come to their senses again. Out of fifty boats, forty-six were sunk, a wonderful performance! I want to go over to them. Now the English battleships are appearing in the bay. They storm in at full speed, cleared for action with their 15-inch guns trained on the remains of my squadron. Now is the time to go to this English admiral to get him to put an end to these acts of hostility. The firing dies away and is gradually silenced. In the background the heavy cruisers are fighting their dying battle. *Seydlitz* capsizes. *Derfflinger* and *Von der Tann* soon have their quarterdeck or forecastle awash; it cannot be much longer before they disappear. Only *Hindenburg* still floats foursquare on the water, although she too rides deeper; I remember that her commanding officer wished to sink her on an even keel to make the disembarkation of the crew more certain. Of the battleships only *Baden* with a list, and *Markgraf*, apparently intact, are still floating. *Emden* floats, as does *Nürnberg*. *Frankfurt* appears to be on the verge of sinking. Then the *Bremse*, taken in tow by an English destroyer, capsizes. Her gallant commander, Oberleutnant-zur-See Schacke, has succeeded in sinking his ship in spite of the English sailors who seized the vessel. On my journey to the English flagship, boats of survivors were also taken in tow.

I was deeply moved and full of thankfulness towards my brave officers and their valiant men, who had carried out the work ordered in such a brilliant fashion. All these wonderful ships and torpedo boats had gone, sunk, once the pride of the German people; mighty work of the German ship-builders' art, how much thought, how much military experiment and experience had been united in them! A development of an importance without equal was here arrested and sunk into the grave.

Alongside the English flagship, which had just anchored, a condition akin to that caused by 'send all boats to the flagship' reigned; patrol boats, drifters, guard boats and ships' boats, all crowded alongside, impatient to announce, to report, that the German fleet had gone to its grave. At last my drifter succeeds in breaking a way for itself and to range alongside. A ladder is put over for me. I step on board the *Revenge* and am met by the English Vice-Admiral, Sir Sydney R. Fremantle[13].

CHAPTER IX

Justification of the scuttling - In prisoner-of-war camps at Nigg, Oswestry, and Donnington Hall - return home

The first part of my duty, the sinking, was completed. Now began the second, to point out the justification for the sinking to the enemy. My chief of staff and I alone held the key to the events of the day.

I started by telling the English admiral that I had caused the fleet to be sunk, and that I alone would be answerable for everything that had happened. The English admiral declared that my action was an 'act of treachery' and told me that I was a prisoner-of-war. A cabin was allotted to me. The reproach of 'treachery' I left unanswered at the time owing to the angry spirit reigning on board; there would yet be time to clear this reproach. I requested the English admiral to allow me my flag-lieutenant, Oberleutnant-zur-See Schilling. It was approved. The starboard side of the quarterdeck was cleared for me. After about ten minutes I was taken to my quarters by a guard of three Royal Marines with fixed bayonets. They were the admiral's cabins on the bridge. My luggage remained untouched.

My flag-lieutenant and I enjoyed the wide view of the now empty Scapa Flow through the big square ports of the Admiral's cabin. Only *Baden* and *Markgraf* and one or two light cruisers were still visible. Not far from us the wreck of the capsized *Seydlitz* towered out of the water. When we again looked out, after about half an hour - it must then have been about four-thirty - at the ships still afloat, we could only see two big white columns of water where the *Markgraf* had been. *Markgraf* must have sunk at this moment. I did not then know what a tragedy had been enacted on board.[14] The commanding officer, Korvettenkapitän Schumann, and two very brave petty officers, fell victims to the murderous bullets of an English drifter coxswain. This man had exceeded the very exact English orders, which were also circulated to us, which were in force for the guarding of the interned squadron, in that he fired at members of the crew of a ship on board their own vessel.

At this time a long signal from the English admiral was being sent to the English squadron from near us on the signal platform. Each word of the signal was called out so loud that we could not fail to hear and understand it if we wanted to or not. In the signal the English officers, amongst other things, were ordered to treat the German crews who had been saved with as much consideration as was consistent with bare humanity, as they had thrown away any right to special consideration by their traitorous conduct; their gear was to be searched thoroughly. That meant in German, therefore, that the men were to be treated as badly as possible and their baggage was to be robbed. My supposition was afterwards confirmed. One or two English ships had at first received the soaked and shivering crews with real consideration; this treatment was then suddenly reversed. Officers and men were badly treated. They had to surrender their baggage and pile it in heaps on the quarterdecks, where it was thoroughly gone through and robbed by the English crews. My cloak fell sacrifice to this plundering on board the battleship *Royal Oak* - I missed it badly in the cold weather there at the time. Today I no longer need it; I present it to its present possessor so that from now on he can boast about his legal ownership before his English friends. I am convinced that it was only because of the financial straits to which the English Empire was reduced, announced as being desperate at the time by the English press, that the English Government did not fulfil their duty of honour in restoring the petty goods and chattels which the German crews had so pitifully saved.

The signal mentioned above induced me now to clear up the reproach of 'treachery.' The English interpreting officer was sent for. I caused the English admiral to be asked, through him, how he arrived at the so-called 'treachery.' Considering our previous relations I could not understand how he could make such a reproach to me. I was of the opinion that war had broken out again. That in accordance with our instructions: 'It is the wish of the All Highest that disabled ships should be sunk,' I was bound to sink the ships. I entreated him not to allow the ships' companies to suffer for what I had ordered. The English admiral sent me his answer through the interpreter, that the good relations between us, speaking not only for himself, but for the other English flag officers as well, was recognised - though only until this day! He was compelled to maintain the reproach of 'treachery' as I had broken the Armistice, which had been extended for two days, that is, until Monday. I thereupon let him be told that I should have been informed by the English Admiralty at once of this extension of the Armistice owing to my isolation from home, that I had no idea of this extension, otherwise the sinking would not have taken place. Due to the fact that the English Admiralty had concealed the extension of the Armistice from me the whole situation was now altered in our favour. The English admiral, through the interpreter, then caused more information to be sought, which I got together to that end as follows: that following the rejection of the German counter-proposals to the peace conditions I had to assume that the state of war would be resumed; the Armistice, I assumed, would cease automatically without previous warning. As I had had no notice of the prolonging of the Armistice period it was my bounden duty, and that too without needing to ask the English admiral for information, to deal with the matter on my own and sink the fleet. News, in so far as I had received any at all, I had gathered from the English press supplied me, and there it was described as 'official.'

It was now dark. After a game of Picquet[15] we, my flag-lieutenant and I, went off to bed. I confess, it was a long time since I spent such a restful night as this. The familiar and what in former days was the friendly noise of the anchor being weighed woke us up. The English squadron of battleships weighed and proceeded from Scapa Flow. When we again came to an anchor it was midday and we were in Cromarty Firth. The English ships, I presume to celebrate the sinking of the German fleet, had dressed ship. A signal from the incoming admiral informed them that this finery was to be hauled down again. At noon the German naval officers were called on to the quarterdeck of *Revenge*. A detachment of Royal Marines with fixed bayonets were fallen in there in a square, further away were the officers and men of the *Revenge*, the commanding officers of the German ships, the leader of the torpedo boats, and my staff were also there – even I received an order to take a part. After a certain time the English admiral appeared. He read out the following speech, which the interpreter translated for us into German:

"Admiral von Reuter!
Before I hand you over to the military authorities I should like to bring to your notice the reasons for my indignation at your act.
This act is contrary to all feelings of propriety and honour. It is a traitorous action, a breach of trust, which you have committed and a disgrace to you!
You have committed an act of war by hoisting your war flag and, at the same time, sinking the ships at a time when the Armistice was in full force.
One sees from this that the spirit of the new Germany is no different from the old. Anyone who has not believed it until now, will now be convinced.
How your act will be understood in your own country is beyond my comprehension.
If you, however, Admiral von Reuter, maintain that the Armistice had expired, this was only based on an unfounded and false assumption.
The letters were just completed and signed by me which would have informed you in accordance with the instructions from my government, whether peace had been signed or not. How could you believe that I would take my squadron to sea for exercises if this day had been such a critical one?
In the same way that Germany started the war by a military treaty violation in the invasion of Belgium, you have ended it by a similar naval violation!
The honour-loving seamen of all nations will be unable to comprehend this act, with the exception perhaps, of yours.
You will now be handed over to the military authorities, who deal with prisoners-of-war."

I could only shake my head during the speech. I had a feeling that the speech was being given on behalf of the reporter of *The Times*, who was present. He must have been on board the English ships already, by Saturday the 21st June, presumably to report on the seizure of the German ships.

This speech, delivered with a background of military pomp, was, of course, meant to represent an important state ceremony. The English revel in such theatrical displays. To the higher standing German mind these displays are in bad taste. To us this treatment appeared to be more in the nature of a film display. It even fell short of the realm of comedy and inspired our compassion. I was sensible to the fact that this theatrical *coup* was uncommonly unpleasant and humbling for the English admiral who appeared to be a sound and high-thinking man.

I answered in German, facing the interpreter: "Tell your admiral that I am unable to agree with the purport of his speech and that our comprehension of the subject differs. I alone carry the responsibility. I am convinced that any English naval officer, placed as I was, would have acted in the same way."

We were then landed. Ashore, a car was placed at my disposal and we drove off through the beautiful Scottish countryside. Trees and bushes stood on either side of the road, and they were green, a long-missed sight!

After about half an hour's run we drove into the camp at Nigg. A Scottish officer led my flag-lieutenant and me to a barrack room. The extensive camp lies in a bay on the slopes of a gradually sloping hill.

High mountains are all around. From our barracks we enjoyed a view over the Scottish Highlands, which are incomparably beautiful. In default of anything else to sit on we settled down on the steps of our barrack room and smoked and waited. 'Waiting' in the days to come was to become our most serious occupation. Gradually the officers and men began to arrive. I could only nod my thanks to them from the distance for their truly loyal fulfilment of duty.

The night was awful and although the Scottish camp commander had produced a bed for me the four blankets supplied were so thin and full of holes that I was bitterly cold in the storm then blowing. At last it was morning. We washed ourselves at the pump and refreshed ourselves on corned beef, nibbled hard bread, waited, and froze.

It was in the camp here that I first learnt how the sinking had been carried out on the individual ships. In the case of *Emden*, *Baden* and *Nürnberg*, the time from when the order was given to the time of seizure by the English was not enough to fill the ships sufficiently to make sure that they would sink. Besides this, on board *Emden*, as I knew already, we were unable to make any large preparation owing to the English dispatch boats constantly lying alongside, whom we feared might discover what was going on. The crew of the battleship *Kaiserin*, after much trouble trying to get a boat out, had to jump overboard before the ship capsized. German boats hurrying to the rescue were in most cases driven away by the English so that the work of rescue was dragged out to half an hour. In spite of this it finally succeeded and all were rescued.

The toll exacted by the irresponsible firing on the part of the English amounted to: 10 killed, including Korvettenkapitän Schumann, commanding officer of the *Markgraf*, and about sixteen wounded, amongst them Staff Engineer Rogge of the *Bayern*.

I take this opportunity of remembering with thankfulness all those various gifts which poured in to me for the survivors and which at least alleviated their most pressing needs.

During the afternoon a car took my chief of staff and me to the railway station, which lay some distance away. The Scottish camp commander accompanied me. His behaviour won my regard.

It must have been about 5 o'clock in the afternoon when we - my staff and I - were lodged in a comfortable and suitable first-class compartment and steamed off to an unknown destination, though a whisper had leaked through early that it was to be Oswestry camp. The night, with the exception of one hour, was as light as day. The journey lay through the middle of the Scottish Highlands; a wonderful trip, which we appreciated.

English newspapers gradually began to reach us, most of them did not remark kindly on the sinking. That was understandable. A few of them, in opposition to this view, did justice to us and expressed themselves as owning our right to the sinking. Had anybody then really been injured by the sinking? Surely the wishes of all parties were fulfilled in a way that is seldom achieved. The pacifists must have rejoiced that a number of nasty war machines were destroyed, the English must have been pleased not to have to worry over the distribution of the ships between her brothers of the Entente, and they, in turn, must have been pleased that England herself could no longer just annex them. And finally, Germany could remain happy in the knowledge that the honour of her navy and at the same time that of the government had been saved.

The English Admiralty, of course, cannot hide a real feeling of shame that this last undertaking of the German fleet was prepared and carried out under the very eyes of the guard boats and truly without it being given away before the appointed time as it happened so many times during the war.

We entered the Oswestry camp during the morning of the 24th June. A car again fetched me from the train and took me straight to the camp commander. He greeted me politely and took my German money from me. The pitifully few pounds I obtained in exchange impressed on me for the first time the depth to which the German exchange value had fallen in a most unpleasant way. A woman driver then drove me to the camp proper. I could hardly recognise her as such at first as the characteristics of her sex, due either to the effect of the U-boat war or to the masculine garments she wore, were effaced. It was not until she removed her cap in the inquiry room that the rich abundance of her hair declared her femininity. She and a 'Tommy' then undertook the examination of the contents of my briefcase.

We were warmly greeted in the camp by Major Nau, the senior officer of the prisoners-of-war, and the other German officers. The comradely fellow-feeling of the Rittmeister von Dresky prompted him to supply me with a sorely missed overcoat. He has no idea how gratefully I thought of him during the next seven months. My cubicle was in a barrack room. Like all barrack rooms, it was cold, draughty though not uninhabitable. The stove had to be kept red-hot day and night in the cold, wet weather then prevailing.

In connection with the sinking, right was on our side. The German Government to start with, as they had absolutely no knowledge of our motives, could take no steps in the matter; we had to take the initiative. I composed a letter to the English Admiralty on that very day. It runs:

24th June 1919.

> I informed the senior British naval officer at Scapa Flow, Vice-Admiral Sir Sydney R. Fremantle, that I, personally and alone, am responsible for the sinking of the interned German ships and torpedo boats.
> The officers and men can therefore not be held answerable for the sinking.
> On these grounds I request that you will again accord, them the privileges due to internees.
> The reason for my not requesting the same advantages for myself is purely a practical one, as I do not want to bring myself into the question as this might endanger the acceptance of this proposal.
> I have sent a copy of this letter to the Swiss Embassy with a request that they will telegraph it to the German Government.

I had requested the interned status to be re-imposed on the German crews – the assumption that war had broken out again was my mistake – as treating them as prisoners-of-war was unauthorised.

Accepting the idea that I would immediately be arraigned before an English judge, I gave no more information on my motives: I did not want to be committed to anything in writing. Further, I proposed that a representative of the Swiss Embassy should be sent to me so that through him, as representing German interests, I could get into touch with the German Government. This proposal came to nothing as unrestricted communication between the embassy and the German Government was not permissible. My stay at Oswestry did not last more than a week. On 30th June the camp commander accompanied me to the concentration camp at Donnington Hall, a castle that lies near the middle of England, in a big park with age-old oaks where all manner of red and fallow deer, rabbits, crows and birds lead a contemplative existence. The transfer to Donnington Hall[16] was no doubt intended to separate me from my officers on account of the forthcoming trial; in that connection the exertions to make certain of my conviction must also have played a part. I had nothing really to complain of in the change except for this difficult parting with my officers.

After a journey of several hours, third class this time, and after numerous changes, we arrived at Donnington Hall amidst the cheers of the German officers. The gates closed behind my flag-lieutenant and myself for seven months. An unexpectedly long time!

The life in a prisoners-of-war camp, whose many sorrows and few joys of captivity have so often been described, need not be gone into in detail here. I found much true and devoted friendship; it was this that brought the sun into the daily greyness of the prisoner's life. The promise that Graf Kageneck, the senior officer in the camp, made me, in the name of all officers on the occasion of their departure from Donnington Hall, was kept to the letter; our departed comrades did not forget we who had been left behind, did not omit to make strenuous efforts to ensure our repatriation and contributed greatly in dispelling our feelings of loneliness in the most understanding and pleasant way by sending us letters and parcels, particularly at Christmas-time. I remember particularly thankfully the demonstration of detached friendship displayed by Gusow, Ruffhold, Duren, Weimar and Bremen. In the camp I had the extreme pleasure of meeting several Coburgers, sons of the town in which I had been brought up, amongst whom I would like particularly to mention the brothers Beck; my conversation with them were the recreation of the day for me. The English camp commander and his officers were thoughtful and kind in their interpretation of the regulations towards me. Nevertheless, I was more carefully watched than my fellow prisoners. My announcement, that I had no thought of escaping, as it would jeopardise the establishment of the justification of the sinking which I wished to impress on England, did not relieve the anxiety of my jailers for a long time.

My thoughts were chiefly concentrated on how I could possibly get a report through to the Admiralty in Berlin. Finally an opportunity presented itself; Leutnant Lobsien, of the reserve of officers, was due to be sent home at the beginning of July to record his vote in Schleswig-Holstein[17]. To entrust a written report to him was too dangerous, so for eight days we hammered away at the report out loud till he knew it by heart; fortunately he hailed from the coast so that naval expressions and terms were familiar to him. By bad luck he was detained in a concentration camp with others awaiting repatriation for four weeks, so he could not deliver my report to the Admiralty in Berlin before the middle of August.

The report was as follows:

Donnington Hall
15th July 1919.

"To the head of the Admiralty.

The reasons for my action at Scapa Flow on 21st June 1919 were the two instructions:

1. A naval commander-in-chief in foreign waters, who is not in touch with the Homeland, is to act on his own initiative as best meets the needs of the State and the honour of the navy.

2. German ships must on no account be allowed to fall into the hands of the enemy in time of war.

The sinking of the interned ships was therefore considered in the case of an attempt at seizure or in case hostilities were resumed due to the peace treaty not being signed. The surrender of the ships was envisaged if the treaty were signed, as it could not be foreseen what consequences the refusal to surrender would have on the sorely pressed German Government, about which I received no information. The necessary orders have already been published, and apparently must have been found out by the English. They cannot be held against me.

On Friday, 20th June, during the afternoon, I learned from *The Times* of 16th June, the official text of the German counter-proposals. In them, the German fleet was to be used as an object of barter. That evening I had a wireless message sent to the German Government requesting that the officers might be relieved of their duty before the surrender.

This wireless message was sent by the first available opportunity to the English admiral in Scapa Flow, Sir S. R. Fremantle, on 21st June for transmission.

After the sending of this message the English newspapers of Tuesday, 17th June arrived. In them was the official text of the final reply of the Entente to the German Government. It contained the refusal to take the interned fleet into consideration as an object of barter, and expressed its absolute refusal of the German counterproposals. In *The Times*, it also said that the German Government was to give a definite answer within five days from the reply to her counter-proposals, and that during the last three days of this five-day respite the Armistice would automatically expire. As this reply was made on 16th June, I had to conclude that if the peace treaty were not signed by Saturday 21st June, a state of war would again be in force. Judging by the tone of refusal of the final note of the Entente and by the speech of the Government spokesman in the German National Assembly and the attitude of the German press, I was entitled to assume that the treaty would not be signed, and therefore that a state of war would be resumed on the Saturday.

I would like to mention in this connection that I received no information of any sort either from the German or the English Governments about the extension of the Armistice period as given in the note of the 16th June, or of any views the German Government held, in general. My only sources of information were the English newspapers, which, as a rule, I received four days after their publication.

In the belief that the state of war had been resumed I gave the order to sink the interned German fleet on Saturday the 21st June.

I first learned of the extension of the Armistice period to Monday the 23rd June, on board the English flagship *Revenge* during the afternoon of the 21st June, through the interpreter to Vice-Admiral Sir S. R.

Fremantle. In my opinion, therefore, no reflection can be cast on me for a violation of the Armistice. The proceedings were then only made possible by the fact that I was isolated from all government news of the Armistice and peace discussions.

I was bound to carry out the sinking in accordance with the order issued at the beginning of the war, which forbade that any German ship should be allowed to fall into the hands of the enemy. It was therefore not a business of the exercise of my own initiative as is represented in the French Prime Minister Clemenceau's note, but rather, solely a proceeding to which I was in duty bound as an officer in accordance with the above quoted government order which has not been cancelled. The sinking only shows my efforts, as good as they could be without any news, to carry out my duty as an officer towards my government.

My order to carry out the sinking was obeyed with the utmost devotion. The actual losses I do not know more certainly than is given by the English press. I want to call special attention to the fact that no armed measures were used against the English military forces and, indeed, due to our lack of weapons this was quite impossible. For this reason there was not a man wounded or killed on the English side, so no act of violence or war was committed against the English armed forces. As regards the sinking it was irrelevant that the greater part of the English guarding force, as was actually the case, had gone to sea. Further, referring to Article 31 of the Armistice conditions, it is only laid down that the material, etc., is not to be destroyed before delivery at the Armistice; what must not be done with the ships after this delivery is not stated. In consequence of this omission, a loophole is left by which alone the sinking can be justified, the more so as it concerns German property and not that of the enemy.

I would like to take this opportunity of acknowledging the practical support accorded me on the part of my chief of staff, Fregattenkapitän Oldekop, and of the leader of the torpedo boats, Korvettenkapitän Cordes.

Leutnant Lobsien of the Reserve acquitted himself of this commission with aptitude and punctuality."

In the middle of July I caused a letter to be sent to the German Government through the representative of the Swiss Embassy, of which only the first paragraph is of interest:

"I beg to state that the repatriation of the crews will probably come about, as the justification for taking them prisoner, the renewal of hostilities, has not in fact taken place. Internment is therefore, now as before, the only permissible measure that can be taken against them: up to the present the internment of the men has really amounted to holding them as prisoners-of-war."

As I had waited several weeks in vain for the password from Leutnant Lobsien to tell me that he had delivered the report at the Admiralty, I decided to send a duplicate of the report direct through the post to the Admiralty in Berlin. My flag-lieutenant, who during all the months at Donnington Hall was a useful helper due to his admirable spirit, character, and a judgment beyond his years, sent this letter to the care of his address.

About the middle of July a wireless message was intercepted in Germany, the text of which was that the proceedings at Scapa Flow were not to be inquired into by the courts. We had also read this in the English press. This wireless message must have misled the government into not taking any steps - at least none as far as we could see - to set forth clearly the justice on the side of Germany in the question of the sinking and to have us set free. As the German Government, including the Admiralty, was absolutely without responsibility for the sinking, they should have demanded my release in order to bring me to trial before their judge. This omission must have had something to do with the attitude the Entente subsequently took up in blaming the German Government for abetting the sinking. Soon after my departure from the Oswestry camp a few individual officers and men were interrogated about the sinking. They confined themselves to the statement that they had done no more than carry out my orders. My legal officer, whom the commission of inquiry sounded most carefully, replied during the discussion on the question of sovereignty over the interned squadron, showing that he was ready to fight the point, that although it was true we had been ordered to haul down our ensigns, yet our 'command' pendants - commissioning pendants and admiral's flag - were left alone and these were the signs of our sovereignty. This was confirmed by the English naval officer assisting at the inquiry by the remark he made to the examining legal official, which was something to this effect: 'There you are, I told you the same thing.' I, myself, was never given a hearing. A court martial was never held: an acknowledgment, therefore, that the Admiralty could find nothing against me nor against the steps I took. A court martial deciding impartially would have exposed England's guilt in isolating the interned squadron from its home authorities and in not informing it of the extension of the period of the Armistice. How far the German Government went in the use of the strength of my position remains unknown to me.

On 24th June the peace treaty was signed by Germany. The repatriation of all the German prisoners-of-war was to follow as soon as the three great powers had ratified the treaty. To judge by the English press that might be delayed for many months yet. The English newspapers, as far as those were concerned who did not absolutely belong to the Northcliffe Group[18], complained that, owing to the bad English financial position where the possibility of every economy ought to be studied, hundreds of thousands of prisoners were still being held in English camps. I studied these reports and came to the conclusion that for financial reasons the English Government would be glad to be rid of the prisoners-of-war - not on your life for reasons of humanity! They were, anyway, in none too strong a position and Lloyd George's nerves seem to have given way, as made more apparent by his extended holiday and the postponement of the economy legislation. On one side the English Government was urged by its own and the vindictive French press to have nothing to do with Germany for settling the question of the prisoners-of-war; on the other side it was assailed by the press of the left and urged to send the hundreds of thousands of prisoners-of-war back to their homes. I decided, therefore, on the strength of being the most senior of the prisoners-of-war in England, to make a preliminary attempt on Lloyd George in the interests of the prisoners-of-war. In this letter I pointed out to him how expensive and how inhumane it was to keep the German prisoners-of-war still captive now that peace had been declared. To make their repatriation dependent on the ratification by the three Great Powers meant a long and unforeseen delay. The tension amongst the German prisoners-of-war was such that any further extension of their captivity was really more than they would be able to endure.

The German Government, in accordance with the peace terms, had nominated a delegate to the Commission for the repatriation of prisoners-of-war immediately after signing the treaty. As, however, close on eight weeks had elapsed since this nomination was made without our becoming aware of any action being taken by this delegate, I was confirmed in the belief that after the action of nominating this delegate with the utmost correctness, the German Government would wait with its hands in its pockets until the Entente or Heaven itself would be benign enough to initiate the repatriation of the prisoners-of-war, so I decided, personally, again to appeal to the German Government. The German press was silent.

The cold attitude of the German Government on the question of repatriation was not only apparent to us prisoners-of-war, as the English camp commander, who at this time - about mid-August - had returned to the camp from the War Office, described his conversations with them to us, whereby the holding back of the prisoners was only due to the German Government. The latter apparently took no interest in the repatriation; the English War Office would have been only too pleased to be rid of the German prisoners-of-war. This news I condensed in the form of a telegram to the German Government. Before I finally sent it off, I forwarded it in the form of a letter through the camp post office addressed to the German press for publication, as without this precaution the telegram would most probably have disappeared without trace into some official's pigeonhole. The telegram was not dispatched to the German Government until it had been received by the press; an English general who happened to stop in the camp, even rewrote it for me in good English so that it would pass the English censors more quickly! It passed through them remarkably quickly and so to the German Government which were offended and began to rage and try to vindicate themselves. We were not served by that alone. A commission was now formed in the camp under the direction of

Kapitän Gillmann, which with much speed, tact, and energy bombarded the German press with propaganda for our repatriation. Every inmate of the camp was to send two letters, one to the Press of his home neighbourhood and the other to the member of the Reichstag representing his constituency, in which he was to complain bitterly that the Press and the government had done nothing towards the repatriation of the prisoners-of-war. Other camps were urged to take similar steps; some had already done so of their own volition. In this way a torrent of complaints were poured over the government and German press and started a storm in the paper world. This perhaps helped in inducing Lloyd George to oppose the French and similar vindictive press concerning the liberation of the prisoners. The removal of my comrades from Donnington Hall was delayed for several weeks more due to the transport strike, which had broken out in England. Not till the end of October did we part from one another. Consequently the German prisoners-of-war may have achieved their release from captivity on their own account by true Baron Munchausen[19] methods. Only we, of the Scapa Flow interned squadron, had yet to endure the hospitality of England for an indefinite time.

The necessary written details of the sinking were again entrusted, this time to a naval officer, containing the same information as the previously described report of 5th July. In this way he would be in a position to inform the Admiralty how the English Government could be influenced by the German press and was then to make certain that real use was made of this. This seemed to me all the more important as the spectre of an indemnity for the sunken fleet was being raised in the English and French newspapers.

I forwarded a protest against our exclusion from the scheme of repatriation to the English Prime Minister. It read:

23rd October 1919.

"To the Prime Minister.

Sir,
I have just learnt that I, Kapitänleutnant Wernig and Oberleutnant-zur -See Schilling, along with six ratings of the German fleet lately interned at Scapa Flow, have been excluded from the general scheme of repatriation of prisoners-of-war to Germany from the camp at Donnington Hall. I conclude from this fact that a similar procedure will be adopted with the remaining officers and men of the interned fleet. This would indicate a breach of the undertaking given by the English Government, that the German prisoners-of-war would be repatriated even before the peace treaty was put into force. Against this exceptional treatment, which would dispense with the elements of justice, reasonableness, and humanity, I wish to record my protest.
I base my protest on the following:
1. As the representatives of the Entente themselves publicly announced

in the Press, the internment of the German fleet was itself a mistake. Neither I, nor my officers and men can be reproached for this mistake, nor is it reasonable to make us suffer for this mistake.

2. The English Government kept me at Scapa Flow, isolated from my government in spite of my protests. I only received written news, under the most favourable circumstances, after an interval of three weeks and wireless messages after several days' delay, that is, insofar as the English censorship allowed them through at all. The English Government should in all honesty, under these circumstances, have kept me currently informed over the progress of the peace negotiations, particularly as far as the notice and termination of the Armistice was concerned.

It is laid down in regulations that I, as commander-in-chief, am bound to deal with any quarrel on my own in the best way in keeping with the needs of the State and the honour of the navy, in all cases of necessity or danger. I received information on the peace negotiations neither from the English nor from my own government, nor could I expect to, latterly, in the short respite where the situation was constantly changing. Consequently the principle of having to act on my own account was, for me, strengthened.

The only sources of information available to me were the English newspapers. Their news was only of importance to me, however, where it was of an official nature and dealt with the (to me) critical days of the 20th and 21st June. This news concerned the German counter-proposals to the peace treaty and the refusal of the former by the Entente. In accordance with the knowledge thus acquired through the English press and the refusal of the German counter-proposals, I concluded, as a certainty, that hostilities would be renewed on 21st June; the German Prime Minister on his part had even declared in the National Assembly that he would rather his hand withered than sign this peace treaty. I could also not think it possible as an officer, that such a treaty could be signed. Danger and war now lay before me; they compelled me, as an officer and man of honour, to act in accordance with my instructions, henceforth independently, to the best of my judgment and conscience. I do not believe that an English naval commander would have had any different instructions nor would he have acted any differently.

3. With a state of war a further regulation came into force as far as I was concerned: "Ships put out of action are not to be allowed to fall into the hands of the enemy." The ships placed under my orders were disabled; the only thing left for me to do was to sink them. That I did. It did not affect my decision in the least whether the greater part of the English guarding forces were at sea or not. I am convinced that English commanders-in-chief have the same instructions and would act as I did.

4. The conclusion I came to, that the war had been resumed on 21st June, was founded on the basis and scrupulous proof of the English newspaper reports before quoted. Yet, although this conclusion of mine later proved to be incorrect, as the newspapers referred to did not mention the two-day extension of the Armistice, I however sank the ships in the firm belief that it was again a time of war. I did not obtain any knowledge of the extended Armistice until the night of 21st June on board HMS *Revenge*. I can never be reproached with a wilful and guilty violation of the Armistice. As we have been declared prisoners-of-war in spite of this, war must apparently have broken out again as I had assumed. We have had to compromise with this. It would now, therefore, be all the more unfair if we were to be deprived of benefiting by the scheme of repatriation now being carried out and treated worse than the prisoners-of-war.

5. If paragraphs 1 to 4 inclusive be appreciated, it will be understood that we now, as we see ourselves excluded from repatriation, feel strengthened in the feeling that we, who, after all, have only carried out our duty, will not be treated with right, fairness, and the chivalry of war, but will be offered purely as a sort of sacrifice to the spirit of revenge. I cannot believe that this is the intention of the English Government.

I therefore request that the discrimination exercised against us in the matter of transporting us home be removed and that my repatriation, as well as that of the officers and men of what was the interned squadron at Scapa Flow, be ordered."

Meanwhile the Entente had actually approached the German Government on the question of an indemnity for the German ships sunk at Scapa Flow. I really thought that the German Government in this case would leave no stone unturned to bring me before a German, international, or English court martial and thereby gain an impartial decision on the question of the sinking. They knew that right was on my side, and I should have been able to testify that I had sunk the ships without the slightest influence from the German authorities being brought to bear on me. I did not understand why the German Government, in this question of compensation, did not stir up the German press with energy; I had particularly impressed upon them the use to which the press might be put. It surely was not agreeable to England that the German naval war material left over should be surrendered, as this would have the effect of re-opening the question of the division of spoils which had been closed, so happily for England, on 21st June. The division amongst the remaining Allies of the harbour materials, by which they would become competitors of England, was also opposed to English interests. The German press had an easy task before it, but indifferently led and not unanimous in its opinions it had to be content with a very varied following in the compensation question. In any case I deny

Above: The 26,947-ton battlecruiser Hindenburg resting on an even keel on the bottom of Scapa Flow. Sinking at 5.00 p.m. on 21st June 1919, Hindenburg was the last capital ship to sink.

The battlecruiser Seydlitz lying on her starboard side after the scuttling on 21st June 1919. A lucky ship, Seydlitz survived massive damage at Jutland, with 22 confirmed large calibre hits.

Above: *Von Reuter's flagship, SMS Emden, beached in Swanbister Bay after the scuttling. This photograph was taken on 23rd June 1919. In the distance you can see the bow of the capsized Bremse.*

Below: *The cruiser SMS Nürnberg, aground on Cava after scuttling.*

Above: *British troops guarding a beached torpedo boat.*

The drifter Ramna, photographed on 23rd June 1919 after running aground on the submerged hull of the SMS Moltke.

Above: The work on salvaging the larger vessels at Scapa Flow began during the spring of 1926 and continued up until the outbreak of World War Two.

Below: Pumping seawater from the Hindenburg during salvage operations in the summer of 1930.

Above: *A salvage worker cutting up the armour plating from one of the German ships*

Below: *Seydlitz after being raised in November 1928, secured alongside Lyness Pier while being prepared for the journey to the breakers at Rosyth.*

Above: One of the diving teams at work during the salvage of the scuttled High Seas Fleet.

Below: Hindenburg demonstrates her alarming tendency to tilt when lifted.

The Bayern, shortly after being raised by Metal Industries in September 1934. The seven towering airlocks would be removed prior to the hull being towed to Rosyth

Above: *Hindenburg, just before being successfully raised by Cox and Danks on 22nd July 1930. The trunk fitted above a forward hatchway was designed to provide an unimpeded flow of air into the hull to replace the water as it was pumped out.*

Salvage workers bringing out souvenirs from one of the German ships.

most emphatically the blame attributed to me for the subsequent surrender of the German harbour material. The hundreds of the Entente's commissions travelling round Germany after the autumn of 1918 must surely have reported that we still had a lot left which could be taken from us to the advantage of the Entente. In order to cloak this robbery it was made out to be a punishment for the Scapa Flow incident, which, accidentally, seemed to offer a better excuse than some arrears or other in the fulfilment of the Treaty of Versailles.

I assured the English Government of the fact that the German Government had not yet been informed of the facts of the sinking in the following letter:

12th December 1919.

"To the Prime Minister of Great Britain and Ireland.

1. I have received no word on the subject of the sinking of the German ships either from the German Government or from any one of its representatives.
2. The letter by the German Rear-Admiral von Trotha, published in the English press could, neither by its wording nor by its implication, have any influence on my way of acting."

A copy of this letter was sent to the German Government.

On the festival day at the end of November I was reunited with my chief of staff and the officers, as well as a number of men, of the interned squadron. We spent two and a half months more of suspense at Donnington Hall, and once again I enjoyed and fully appreciated that which is held locked up, through things held in common in a united body of officers, in their spirit, in their feeling of comradeship and in their tireless enthusiasm for their profession. The naval corps of officers thus seemed to me to be the last and noblest blood of that which the much decried but yet so very prosperous militarism of the Hohenzollerns put into motion.

In the last days of January the hour of our freedom struck. On 29th, just after midnight, the prison doors of Donnington Hall were opened. A special train brought us to Hull. There lay the German steamer in which we were to embark and which was to take us to Wilhelmshaven.

Harsh and unrecognisable was the passage from victorious England, the country where patriotism, order, and cleanliness ruled and where a man's standing was taken for granted, to beaten Germany. Even the steamer gave one an idea of the low state to which Germany had sunk. Still, it was going homewards. On the night of 29th January the anchor was weighed and we left Hull.

After a voyage of a day and a half we steered into the mouth of the Jade by the grey light of dawn. Once again, and for most of us probably for the last time, the North Sea had shown herself to us in all her harsh beauty. Sky and sea grey and hard, misty the horizon: like our future! A long swell made our steamer pitch and roll heavily. In the Jade the iron flotilla saluted us, a first welcome greeting! At noon we entered the lock at Wilhelmshaven to the strains of the Admiral's musical honours. The head of the Admiralty, the officers of the station, members of the war associations, detachments of troops, and the inhabitants of the towns of Wilhelmshaven and Rustringen all bade us a friendly welcome.

The day of homecoming brought reunion with all the good comrades who had shared sorrow and happiness for so many long months. 'Dead is that friendly distress…' For many now commenced that struggle for existence in a new calling. But few were selected to serve their land further in the Reichswehr Navy. They know that the sinking of the fleet only represents a portion of their duty. The other, greater – its reconstruction – lies before them. Whether it will be their lot to survive the first birth pangs of the third German fleet, who can today say? But yet their duty will be fulfilled if they bear a share in maintaining the splendid spirit of the second German navy, that wonderful, vigorous fleet which off the Skagerrak belied the hundred-year-old saying: 'Britannia rules the waves.'

Unconquered it lies in the harbour of Scapa Flow sunk in its self-chosen grave.

God-speed the third German fleet!

Von Reuter's Legacy

Reclaiming the Imperial navy

*F*rom Admiral von Reuter's stirring sentiment: "God-Speed the third German fleet!" at the end of his account of the scuttling of the High Seas Fleet it is clear that even so soon after the humiliation of defeat he was defiantly contemplating the day when the German navy would once again be a force to be reckoned with.

Meanwhile, the remains of the Kaiser's High Seas Fleet lay, apparently forgotten and rusting, at the bottom of Scapa Flow. Perhaps von Reuter can be forgiven for assuming that the adventure was over as the waters of Scapa Flow settled above the remains of the German fleet; indeed, following the scuttling Britain was also determined to draw a veil over the incident and leave the ships to rust where they lay. As far as the Admiralty was concerned, with the exception of the battleship *Baden*, the light cruisers *Emden*, *Frankfurt* and *Nürnburg* and eighteen destroyers which were either beached or sunk in relatively shallow water, the remaining ships of the former High Seas Fleet were now out of sight and quite definitely out of mind.

The locals, on the other hand, felt differently. The submerged hulks were creating shipping hazards and in October 1920, the Aberdeen trawler *Ben Urie* ran hard on to the wreck of the *Moltke* and remained fast for several hours until the flood tide enabled her to float off. The *Ben Urie* was by no means the first vessel to run foul of the *Moltke* and it was not long before the local press began to call for the Admiralty to have the wrecks properly marked.

At first their entreaties fell on deaf ears, but when a local salvage syndicate succeeded in raising a destroyer in 1922, before towing it to Stromness for scrapping, officials at the Admiralty began to alter their opinion. By the following summer the Admiralty had sold four destroyers to the Scapa Flow Salvage and Shipbreaking Company, headed by J.W. Robertson, who also happened to be leader of Shetland County Council. In the event, however, Robertson would not raise his first vessel until August 1924, by which time he was facing formidable competition from Ernest Cox, a man who would ultimately become a legend at Scapa Flow.

The story is all the more remarkable because Cox, although a successful engineer and scrap metal merchant, initially had absolutely no experience in the field of marine salvage. Nevertheless, after the end of the war he concluded that with the growing need for scrap metal, there was considerable money to be made in ship-breaking. In 1921 he purchased the battleships *Orion* and *Erin* from the Admiralty, each at a cost of £25,000 and proceeded to dismantle them at his breakers' yard on the Isle of Sheppey, and at the conclusion of the operation he had more than doubled his money.

Marine salvage, however, required quite different skills and marked a major departure even for him. Nevertheless, in February 1924, having inspected the scuttled warships he returned to the Admiralty and purchased no less than twenty-six destroyers and the battleships *Seydlitz* and *Hindenburg* for the princely sum of £24,000.

What Cox lacked in experience he more than made up for in initiative, application and hard work, and in order to gain knowledge and practical skills, he started on the smaller 900-ton destroyers. He began by cutting a floating dock in half and running steel cables beneath the sunken hulks, which were then secured above to the floating docks. The cables were pulled tight at low water, and as the tide came in both docks would rise, pulling the wreck up with them. At high tide the platforms were moved towards the shore until the wreck grounded. At the next low tide the cables were again pulled tight and the process repeated. This technique even worked for righting capsized vessels, which could cause numerous problems when parts of the submerged superstructure, masts or guns became snagged on the seabed. By paying out the cable a few feet on one side and taking up the slack on the other, an inverted hull would by these means usually roll naturally into an upright position. The superstructure could then be removed after the wreck had been beached,

The first wreck to be raised on 1st August 1924 was the torpedo boat *V70*, but rather than sell it for scrap Cox, instead, refitted it as a carpenter's workshop and named it *Salvage Unit 3*. His anger, however, knew no bounds when he discovered that *V70*'s deck torpedo tubes, which were made from valuable gunmetal, had already been surreptitiously removed and sold off by some of the local fishermen sometime before.

He went on to successfully raise another five torpedo boats before the end of the year, and by the summer of 1925 he had recouped half of his original £45,000 investment. In spite of the fact that Cox never worked his men on a Sunday, it only took him twenty months to raise twenty-five destroyers, totalling 23,000 tons. Fourteen vessels were raised in 1925 alone, while the last torpedo boat, *G104*, was successfully raised on 30th April 1926.

With the minnows now all accounted for, Cox was finally free to turn his attention to the big prizes.

The battlecruiser *Hindenburg* seemed to be the most obvious and attractive target. Lying in seventy-feet of water and the only capital ship resting on an even keel, Cox considered two potential salvage procedures. The first was a variation on the tried and tested winch and tide technique which had proved to be so successful for the torpedo boats, but using four docks instead of two as well as air bags for additional flotation. The problem with this method, however, was that while it was adequate for a 1,500-ton torpedo boat, a much heavier battlecruiser of 27,000-tons was an altogether different matter. Even if it were to work, the available facilities at Lyness in Orkney were only suitable for dismantling the small torpedo boats, and still left him with the problem of having to make the wreck watertight before towing to the Rosyth shipyards for dismantling.

He, therefore, considered a further technique which would involve freezing over the openings in the hull and bringing it to the surface using compressed air. This method seemed to offer the greatest guarantee of success, but the expensive freezing procedure was abandoned in favour of the manufacture of specially made patches. After divers had sealed off all of the valves inside the wreck using quick-drying cement, Cox's shore-based workshops worked on wood and metal patches created from templates manufactured by the dive teams in the water. The porthole patches were usually the simplest and could be bolted to the hull reasonably easily. The caissons and oval-shaped funnel openings, however, proved to be a lot more complicated and it finally took a team of sixteen divers five months to manufacture the patches and make the hull airtight.

By the summer of 1926 Cox was ready to lift the vessel. With a trunk fitted over the forward hatchway leading to the surface in order to guarantee a constant airflow, the pumping finally began, and for five days it continued at a rate of 3,600 tons of water per hour. Slowly the water level inside the hull could be seen to be dropping and when *Hindenburg* started to move Cox could confirm that neutral buoyancy had finally been re-established. Slowly the keel floated free from the seabed, but as the bow continued to rise, very slowly the ship began to heel to port. Before too long the angle of roll was almost forty degrees and realising that if he continued with the operation there was every chance that *Hindenburg* would roll over and capsize altogether, he decided to let her down again and reposition the pumps so that she could be raised stern first instead.

The second attempt proved to be no more successful, even though a floating dock had been placed along the ship's starboard side with numerous nine-inch cables to arrest the anticipated list. Realising that to continue the operation would not only endanger the floating dock but also everyone on it, Cox abandoned the lift and went back to the drawing board,

Reasoning that a combination of shingle and hard rock on the seabed beneath the *Hindenburg* was preventing the ship's bow or stern from digging in, and the fact that the *Hindenburg* was too heavy on one side meant that it would be almost impossible to balance the ship on her three-foot keel. Cox concluded that the only way to offset the problem was to correct the balance, and he decided that an effective way to achieve this was to attach one of the refloated torpedo boats to *Hindenburg*'s high side as the ship became buoyant, and then flood the interior of the destroyer to increase the weight on the higher starboard side until the hull became level.

By September they were ready to try again. For a third time *Hindenburg* began to rise and as soon as the hull had come up to the desired level the torpedo boat was secured alongside and water pumped into its hull. The procedure appeared to be working. *Hindenburg* was still listing, but this time only at an angle of five degrees. However, as the upper deck began to break the surface once again she began to tilt alarmingly to almost twenty-five degrees. Additional cables were attached from the floating dock, but any chance of saving the operation was lost when the weather deteriorated and a gale began to blow, with cables and securing lines breaking loose. Finally, when the boiler powering the pumps on the floating dock broke down Cox knew that to proceed was futile. Ordering the salvage crews to "let her down," all he could do was watch as his men swarmed aboard to retrieve the pumps before *Hindenburg* sank to the bottom for the fourth time, taking with her all his profit of £30,000 and more, which he had made from the salvage of the torpedo boats.

It had been Cox's original intention to go back and raise *Hindenburg* in the spring of 1927, but it would be another four years before he finally returned to the object of his undoing. Showing little regard for the huge financial setback he had suffered, he stoically moved on to his next target, the battleship *Moltke*.

The 23,000-ton *Moltke* was a very different proposition to *Hindenburg*, and in that she lay in over seventy feet of water off the western shore of Cava, she presented Cox with an altogether different technical challenge. Continuing to believe that compressed air was still the best way to go about the task, Cox immediately arranged for his divers to start patching all the known openings to the vessel. By 26th October this chore had been completed and with everything on course for the *Moltke* to be beached on Cava by Christmas, it would seem that he had put the disaster surrounding the *Hindenburg* well and truly behind him.

Cox knew that the underlying procedure was sound, and if the hull could be made watertight then it could be pumped from the surface until the increased internal air pressure would restore its positive buoyancy, at which point the vessel would float to the surface. By November enough compressors had been amassed to pump 300,000 cubic feet of air in twenty-four hours, and after removing the propellers to lighten the load the pumps were started.

To begin with, the procedure worked almost perfectly. Slowly the *Moltke's* submerged hull began to pull itself free of the mud, but in so doing it developed a list of thirty-three degrees to port. It seemed to be a repeat of the *Hindenburg* problem all over again, but in reality it was something that Cox had anticipated, and although he conceded that it would now be impossible to have the hull beached by Christmas, he knew exactly what had to be done. The fact that *Moltke* was coming up by the bow was forcing all of the free air to collect in the highest part of the hull, until it reached the point where the pressure would would force out the volume of air from the higher end. In order to better control the raising process, Cox reasoned that if the inside of the hull were to be divided into three sections, each could then be filled separately with as little or as much air as was required to better control the ascent.

For the salvage crews, this entailed working in appalling conditions inside the hull of the upturned battleship, some fifty feet beneath the surface. In order to succeed, Cox constructed a number of extended air locks, which were designed to protrude six feet above the normal high tide level in the Flow. These tubes were fabricated from a sequence of disused steel boilers, each about six feet wide and twelve feet in length. Entry hatches and an access ladder were then fitted to either end of the tube. Once the airlock tube had been bolted into place and the compressed air pipe that would allow the men to work inside the tube had been fitted the work of cutting into the hull could finally begin.

Two airlock tubes were set in place and by the time the pumps had created an internal air space of some ten feet the first crews were able to go inside the hull to begin the work of sealing off the three sections. It was especially hazardous for the divers, working to seal the openings beneath the water level inside the inverted engine rooms where there were fallen boilers and mountains of coal. Other crews, without diving suits, were able to work inside the hull to seal off the side tanks in the dry sections of the bulkhead. At first they had to cut doors so that they could gain access to the entire length of the hull. At all times the lives of the crews working in *Moltke's* upturned hull were totally dependent on the ability of those on the pontoons to keep the compressors running. Failure to maintain adequate air pressure would have caused the hull to flood in minutes and there would have been no escape for the men trapped inside.

In spite of the punishing conditions, by May of 1927 the task of sealing off the interior was complete. Even though he could now raise the hull, either by its stern or bow, Cox needed to correct the thirty-three degree roll to port as the vessel surfaced. Learning from his experience with the *Hindenburg*, a salvaged torpedo boat was secured to the starboard side of the hull and partially flooded, while twenty nine-inch cables running from the two largest floating docks were shackled to the centre line of the hull in the vicinity of the gun turrets. As the tide began to turn the cables were pulled taught and the compressors were run up to full power to increase the internal pressure. As the hull slowly began to rise the list to port became evident, but not nearly as heavily as before. Disaster loomed once again when five of the cables parted with explosive force, and fearing that the others would follow Cox ordered the remaining cables to be released. This still left the hull with a twenty-two degree list, and when divers reported that the cables had not snapped under the load, but had actually been cut through by the sharp edges of the ship's deck, the cables were re-attached, this time with specially manufactured metal pads to act as cushions between the wires and the hull.

At low tide on 10th June 1927 the process began once again and *Moltke's* bow was pumped to full pressure. As the bow surfaced it again began to list by some sixteen degrees, but this was nothing like as as severe as before and by the time that the slack in the cables had been taken up, the list had been reduced to just three degrees. At 1.15 p.m. the hull now came alive as the stern floated clear of the seabed and a few minutes later the stern surfaced amidst a rush of water spouts and gushing air, setting the docks rolling. By the time the turbulence had subsided, the upturned hull of the *Moltke* was floating serenely on the surface, and almost completely level.

Cox had finally achieved his goal, but his trials were still not quite over. As the *Moltke* was being towed to the shore one of the dangling central eleven-inch guns jammed into the seabed, requiring the floating docks to be repositioned so that divers could go below and cut away the offending protrusion. In spite of this last setback the *Moltke* was now tantalisingly close to the shore and there could be no disguising Cox's achievement. The battleship was eventually beached beside the pier at Lyness, but because the facilities there were totally inadequate for dismantling such a large vessel, after being made watertight and seaworthy *Moltke* was eventually towed 275 miles south to the breaking yards of the Alloa Shipbreaking Company at Rosyth.

Cox's next targets were the battleships *Seydlitz* and *Kaiser*. *Seydlitz* presented him with a particularly interesting challenge as she lay on her starboard side. In 1926 this had been something of a blessing to Cox, as the ship's port side coalbunker had provided him with a virtually limitless supply of coal during a time when the General Strike had caused its cost to reach the ruinous price of over £2 per ton. This abundant supply of 'local' fuel enabled him to keep his salvage crews working throughout the entire strike. By 1928 with her salvage imminent, *Seydlitz's* orientation was considerably less of an advantage. The hull lay in twelve fathoms of water, and at low tide it could be, and on occasion was, mistaken for an island. Cox had succeeded in raising the inverted *Moltke*, but the challenge of lifting a 25,000-ton hull that lay on its side was far more daunting. Nevertheless, that is exactly what he decided to do.

At first the task was very similar to the operations carried out on *Hindenburg* and *Moltke*. Each of the openings in the hull were patched by divers, while salvage crews worked inside the pressurised hull to reinforce and seal the bulkheads. Their labour was long, but by the summer of 1928 work was nearing completion. Cox now determined that the time was right to raise the *Seydlitz*, but as the hull began to rise a series of muffled detonations from within testified to the collapse of one of the forward bulkheads. This resulted in a rush of compressed air into the over-inflated bow of the ship, completely destroying the stability of the hulk, and in a few seconds nine-months of hard labour had come to nothing as *Seydlitz* rolled over and again sank beneath the surface.

This setback would prove to be very costly, but far from being daunted by the prospect, Cox simply restarted work on the hull the very next day. Instead of lying on her side, *Seydlitz* was now resting on her upper works at an angle of forty-eight degrees, which, although considerably more than the seventeen degrees of the *Moltke*, effectively made the salvage a lot simpler than before. Work immediately began on resealing the hull and repositioning the airlocks, and for the next three months the crews set about repairing the internal damage caused by the its sudden capsize. By the beginning of October *Seydlitz* was once again deemed to be ready, but as the pumps were switched on and the hull began to rise with a tilt of some thirty degrees it was clear that it was still unstable. The ship was allowed to gently return to her original position and by locating a concrete pier made from old steel boilers filled with quick-drying cement beneath the lower side of the ship, Cox was finally able to keep the hull level and from there he could work on rebalancing it until it was ready to be lifted.

By the end of October, after a series of experimental lifts, the list had been reduced to twenty-five degrees and Cox decided that the time was now right for yet another try. Positioning the large floating dock above the starboard side of the hull, twenty-two nine-inch steel cables were attached to it to give as much support as possible on the heavier starboard side. Gradually the pressure inside began to build and the ship slowly rose at the bow with no discernible list. All seemed to be going according to plan when the stern suddenly lurched upwards. As *Seydlitz* broke the surface there was a series of ten loud reports as one cable after another broke, but then they stopped abruptly. The fact that the remaining cables were still intact could mean only one thing – *Seydlitz* was floating! Not only that, but she was only recording a list of eight degrees. The subsequent tow to Lyness was not without its hazards and an ebbing neap tide caused her to ground when only three miles from safety, but it was only a temporary delay and within a week she was safely secured alongside the Lyness pier.

The costly lessons learned through his work on the *Hindenburg*, *Moltke* and *Seydlitz* meant that by the time Cox was turning his attention to the 24,700-ton *Kaiser*, he was exhibiting rather more caution than before. Work on the *Kaiser* had been continuing in parallel for many months prior to the raising of the *Seydlitz*, but with the winter now setting in it would not be until the spring of 1929 that he would choose to make his first attempt. Nevertheless, after taking every precaution *Kaiser*'s lift on 20th March went without any problems whatsoever – save for one young electrician who received the fright of his life when he found himself inside the hull during the ascent.

After his great success with the *Kaiser*, it seems curious that having gained so much experience with the larger ships, Cox would instead turn his attention to the 4,385-ton light cruiser *Bremse*. On the day of the scuttling the *Bremse* had capsized while under tow when she was only yards from the shore. The wreck presented Cox with an interesting challenge as her bow was above the surface while her stern lay at a depth of eleven fathoms. The practice of sealing off the bulkheads was carried out in the customary way, but rather than attempting to raise her on her side and risk undoing all of the work, as he had experienced on the *Seydlitz*, Cox instead had the superstructure blown away so that the hull could be fully inverted. The lifting process was basically a return to the technique that had proved so successful with the torpedo boats, and through a combination of compressed air and cables run beneath the hull and pulled tight at low tide, *Bremse* was successfully flipped over and refloated on 27th November.

This effectively marked the end of active operations for 1929, and Cox, with his financial position now restored and with many technical lessons thoroughly learned, was once again planning to take on the monster into which he had effectively sunk some £40,000 of his personal fortune.

It had always been Cox's desire to raise the *Hindenburg* on her keel, and although he conceded that this might not be possible, he still wanted to try and do it as originally planned. This time he decided to cut away much of the surviving bridge structure and remove the forward B turret. To further prevent the hull from rolling he partially raised it and placed a wedge, fabricated from a thirty-foot section of an old-concrete-filled torpedo boat and positioned it beneath *Hindenburg's* port quarter. Meanwhile, two cofferdams were also constructed on either side of the ship to house additional six-inch pumps that were capable of removing some three hundred tons of water per hour. In spite of the passage in time of more than three years over sixty percent of the patches put in place during the summer of 1926 were still considered to be sound, although the extra work would still take a further six months and cost him considerably more. Finally, by July 1930 he was ready for one more attempt.

At first all went well. Within hours *Hindenburg's* hull had risen ten feet and, more importantly, she was level. The cofferdam pumps were then switched on and she continued to rise, but then, with the bow having risen by a total of sixteen feet, the first telltale signs of a starboard list could be detected. As the list gradually increased Cox was reluctantly forced to switch off the compressors and once again let the hull settle back onto the seabed. This time, however, he was confident that he could solve the problem. Ordering another wedge to be positioned beneath *Hindenburg's* starboard quarter, he took a hard-earned rest for three weeks.

On his return they were ready to try again. With the new wedge in position and the pumping arrangements slightly reconfigured, Cox once more ordered pumping to restart. *Hindenburg's* bow began to rise and by the time it had reached a height of sixteen feet it was still level. He knew well that he could only be sure of the success of his plan after pumping of the stern section had begun and the propellers had risen clear of the two concrete wedges supporting the hull. At first the omens were not good as a list developed of over six degrees to port. But then the needle on the indicator stopped moving and seemed to stay fixed for breath-taking moments before slowly moving back. As the indicator watchman began to call out the decreasing list Cox knew that he'd finally beaten the bane of his salvaging career. By the late afternoon of 22nd July 1930, after twelve years resting on the bottom of Scapa Flow, the 27,000-ton battlecruiser, the largest vessel ever lifted from the seabed, was afloat and on a completely even keel.

Aside from the fact that he had achieved an amazing feat of engineering, the substantial scrap value of the *Hindenburg* still left Cox with an overall deficit of £20,000 on his seven-year investment in Scapa Flow. Reasoning that one more year of operations would suffice to make him break even, he decided to continue the work. Having already surveyed the hulls of the battlecruiser *Von der Tann* and the battleship *Prinzregent Luitpold*, he firmly believed that this was not an unrealistic target, and by September of that year the first airlock had already been put in position on the *Von der Tann*.

A serious explosion inside the battlecruiser when an oxy-acetylene torch ignited an undetected gas pocket slowed the operations, but while Cox considered himself fortunate that no one had been killed, additional safety precautions slowed the progress of the salvage. Nevertheless, by 7th December

Von der Tann had been successfully beached on Cava.

By the end of 1930, following the onset of the Depression the value of scrap metal had plunged and Cox's intention to sell off the 20,000-tons realised by the successful salvage of the *Von der Tann* was destined to wait. Matters had not improved substantially by the summer of 1931, by which time the 25,000-ton *Prinzregent Luitpold* had also been salvaged and it would not be until 1933 by which time the price of scrap metal had begun to recover, that the hulks of these last two vessels would finally be towed south to Rosyth for dismantling.

By this time Cox had decided that his adventure at Scapa Flow was coming to an end. A combination of family pressures and the accidental death of an employee in a mysterious explosion on the *Prinzregent Luitpold* convinced him that the desire to break even should no longer be a priority. His accumulated financial loss following eight years of work at Lyness was still in the region of £10,000, although it should be said that the personal financial deficit he experienced at Scapa Flow was more than compensated for by revenue gained from his other flourishing business activities, leaving him a very wealthy man.

After salvaging the *Prinzregent Luitpold* Ernest Cox took no further part in the work at Scapa Flow. At the end of 1932 he sold his remaining assets at Lyness to the Alloa Shipbreaking Company, formerly his principal client in the sale of the salvaged wrecks. Almost immediately this company, renamed Metal Industries, would pick up where he left off, utilising many of the techniques that Cox had so successfully pioneered.

The first battleship to be raised by Metal Industries was the 28,500-ton *Bayern*, which would have been Cox's next target had he continued his own operations. Nevertheless, even though Metal Industries were using tried and tested equipment, along with much of Cox's experienced workforce, they also had their reverses. On one occasion *Bayern* unexpectedly shot to the surface when a compressed air pipe inside the hull burst, wrenching a number of the ship's gun turrets free in the process. *Bayern* was quickly allowed to return to her temporary resting place until 1st September 1934, when the internal work was finally completed and she was brought safely to the surface.

The value of the scrap metal retrieved from the *Bayern* added £110,000 to the coffers of Metal Industries, although with Europe in the early stages of rearmament this meant that the demand for scrap metal and armour plate was suddenly that much greater. Thereafter Metal Industries continued to raise one battleship a year starting with the *König Albert* 31st July 1935; the *Kaiserin*, 11th May 1936; the *Friedrich der Grosse*, 29th April 1937; the *Grosser Kurfürst*, 29th April 1938 and, finally, von Reuter's old ship, the *Derfflinger*, in August 1939. Ironically, much of the steel and armour plate from the Kaiser's High Seas Fleet almost certainly found its way back to customers in Germany to be incorporated into the fast expanding Kriegsmarine, and it is entirely possible that some elements of the High Seas Fleet may even have found their way into the new super battleships being built in Germany prior to World War II.

By September 1939, however, it was too late to have any soul-searching concerns about who was buying the steel and for what purpose. Following the outbreak of the Second World War, all work on further salvage operations was suspended for its duration. In fact, Metal Industries would never pick up from where they left off. In 1946 the upturned *Derfflinger* was finally towed to the Clyde for dismantling, but for the three remaining battleships *König, Kronprinz Wilhelm* and *Markgraf*, and the four light cruisers *Brummer, Cöln, Dresden* and *Karlsruhe*, the commercial viability of raising these wrecks was not particularly strong in a post-war world already awash with scrap metal. As a result, they remain on the seabed to this day, a testament to von Reuter's honour to his beloved High Seas Fleet and to his country, and a source of profound historical interest to scuba divers from all over the world.

In 1957 the Royal Naval base at Scapa Flow was finally closed. Although the legions of naval personnel and salvage workers are now long gone, limited salvage is still carried out from time-to-time, especially as the wrecks have proved to be a valuable source of steel made prior to the arrival of the atomic bomb. Steel manufactured before 1945 contains lower levels of radiation and the metal resting on the seabed at Scapa Flow has considerable value for the manufacture of specialised scientific instruments for measuring levels of radioactivity, and for lining radiation-free compartments of nuclear installations.

In that many thousand of tons of steel still remain resting on the seabed at Scapa Flow, perhaps the salvage story still has another chapter to run. If one were to also consider for a moment the enormous amount of inward investment brought about by sixteen years of almost uninterrupted salvage activity between 1924 and 1939, as well as its focus as a marine tourism attraction, it would seem that Admiral von Reuter's decision to scuttle his fleet, while ultimately intended as a last gesture of defiance, may actually have turned him into a one of the biggest benefactors that Orkney has ever known.

Perhaps that is the greatest irony of all?

ADDITIONAL NOTES

1. In 1761, during the Seven Years War, Prussian Junker Johann Friedrich Adolf von der Marwitz (1723-1781) was ordered to sack Hubertusbug Castle in Saxony, in retaliation for local plundering. In the militaristic world of Frederick the Great's army, obedience and duty was a cardinal rule of the Prussian elite but for von der Marwitz the order ran counter to his own personal code of honour. He refused to carry out the order, knowing that such a refusal could only result in the ruin of his military career. A stone was later placed in the church at Friedersdorf Gedenkstein, which said: "He selected disgrace, where obedience did not bring honour." Coincidentally, the treaty ending the Seven Year's War between Prussia and Austria was signed at Hubertusburg on 15th February 1763.

2. The Convention of Tauroggen was signed following the retreat from Moscow on 30th December 1812, between the Prussian General Yorck and Russian General von Diebitsch. Yorck, along with 17,000 Prussian troops and sixty guns, had been an integral part of Napoleon's Grande Armée, which had invaded Russia in June 1812. By signing the Convention Yorck and his men effectively became neutrals, and so far as Napoleon was concerned his desertion was always an act of the basest treachery. It also paved the way for the War of German Liberation in 1813, and within the year Napoleon had finally been forced back to the French frontier.

3. Rear-Admiral Hugo Meurer was born on 28th May 1869 at Sallach, Saxony. He joined the Imperial Navy in 1886 and during the war served as captain of the pre-dreadnought *Deutschland* at the Battle of Jutland, and the battleship *König* from 14th July 1916 to 23rd May 1917. In May 1917 he was promoted to the rank of Konteradmiral (Rear-Admiral) and made second in command of the 4th Battle Squadron, during which time he took part in a naval expedition to the Baltic between 21st February to 2nd May 1918. He served in this post until 30th July 1918, when he was promoted to Temporary Commander of the 4th Battle Squadron, with the promotion being made permanent on 13th August. He would retain this post until the Armistice, when he was selected as the German naval plenipotentiary to discuss the Armistice terms with the British. Meurer had also been considered to command the interned squadron but his appointment as a delegate to the Armistice Commission in Wilhelmshaven ensured that the post ultimately went to von Reuter.
    Following the signing of the Treaty of Versailles, Meurer retired from the German Navy with the rank of Vizeadmiral (Vice-Admiral) in 1920 and died on 4th January 1960 in Kiel.

4. Helgoland (in English, Heligoland) is a small triangular-shaped island approximately two kilometers in length, though a smaller island east of it is usually also included. The islands are located in the Heligoland Bight or German Bight in the south-east corner of the North Sea, seventy kilometres from the German mainland: the populated 1.0 km2 main island of Hauptinsel lies to the west, and the Düne to the east, which at 0.7 km2 is somewhat smaller. The two islands are a part of the Pinneberg district of the German State of Schleswig-Holstein.
    The islands were Danish property from 1714 until seized by the British in 1807 during the Napoleonic Wars. Britain gave the islands to Germany in 1890, as well as ceding their interests in Madagascar to the French, in return for those countries giving up any claim to the African island of Zanzibar (now a part of Tanzania), largely so the

110

British could intervene there to suppress the slave trade.

Under the German Empire the islands became a major naval base and during the First World War the civil population was evacuated to the mainland. The first naval engagement of the war, the Battle of Heligoland Bight was fought nearby on 28th August 1914, when the British scored a clear victory, sinking the German light cruisers *Mainz*, *Cöln* and *Ariadne*, as well as the destroyer *V187*.

5. On 17th November 1917 Reuter was involved in an engagement with a British squadron while leading a mine sweeping operation with four cruisers and ten destroyers. Attacked by an overwhelmingly superior force, including battleships and battlecruisers, his rearguard action resulted in the loss of only one trawler. His strategy was to lead the attacking force into a minefield but the British broke off the action just in time. During the action Reuter's flagship, SMS *Königsberg*, took a direct hit from a fifteen-inch shell that failed to explode. It remained a family trophy for many years after the war.

6. The Battle of the Skagerrak is the German name for the Battle of Jutland, which was fought on 31st May 1916. The German High Seas Fleet under the command of Vice Admiral Reinhard Scheer attempted to force an action with a part of the British Fleet under conditions of local German superiority. The operation was originally conceived as a bombardment of Sunderland by the German battlecruisers in order to draw out the battlecruisers of Admiral Sir David Beatty, based at Rosyth. Once the isolated British squadron was under the guns of the entire High Seas Fleet they would then be annihilated, but a combination of technical problems and bad weather meant that the attack on Sunderland was cancelled in favour of an expedition towards the Skagerrak on 31st May. Coincidentally, a major operation of the British Grand Fleet had been planned for the beginning of June but a number of intercepted German transmissions persuaded the Admiralty that the High Seas Fleet was planning a major offensive, and by the evening of 30th May the Grand Fleet was already at sea.

Reuter's somewhat biased appreciation of the battle is understandable. The High Seas Fleet inflicted more damage on the Grand Fleet than it suffered itself; the British lost three battlecruisers three cruisers, one light cruiser and seven destroyers, whereas the Germans lost one pre-dreadnought battleship (*Pommern*), one battlecruiser (*Lützow*), four light cruisers and four destroyers. When you also take into account the fact that the British lost 6,097 men killed as opposed to the 2,551 German dead, the German claim of a tactical victory is therefore not without foundation. Leaving aside the official figures, however, the fact that many of the surviving ships of the High Seas Fleet were badly mauled and had broken off the battle to return to port told a very different story. It would never re-emerge to seriously challenge the Grand Fleet again, so ultimately the strategic outcome of the battle can only be looked upon as a British victory.

7. The Pentland Firth lies between the northern Scottish mainland and the Orkney Islands. This stretch of water has a well-deserved reputation among the world's mariners as a particularly treacherous channel - the tide surges through the Firth from the Atlantic to the North Sea and back again twice every day, and the currents can reach up to twelve knots. The Firth itself is not large - around seventeen miles from Dunnet Head, which serves as its westerly entrance, to the most easterly of the islets that make up the Pentland Skerries to the east. The gap between Caithness on the mainland and Orkney varies from six to eight miles, and the islands of Stroma and Swona lie in the channel. The lighthouse on the Skerries (erected in 1794) was the fifth modern lighthouse to be built in Scotland.

8. "They exchanged what they possessed for that which they thought most necessary for the heightening of their joy in life. The article most in demand everywhere was brandy, which in spite of all orders to the contrary we had on board regrettably in excessive quantity due to the administration of the Soldiers' Councils, whilst we lacked soap and tobacco almost completely." [Ludwig von Reuter]

9. Charles Maurice de Talleyrand (1754–1838): French statesman and diplomat. Born into the high nobility he was early destined for the Roman Catholic Church because of a childhood accident that left him partially lame. In 1789 King Louis XVI appointed him Bishop of Autun, but that same year Talleyrand sided with the revolutionaries following the 1789 revolution. In 1792 he was sent by the National Assembly on a mission to London to secure Great Britain's neutrality, but the radical turn of the French Revolution nullified his success and as a lifelong supporter of a Constitutional Monarchy he sought refuge in England. In 1794 he went to the United States, where he remained until the establishment of the Directory in France, returning to Paris in September 1796. The following year he became the French Foreign Secretary, but with a keen eye on future political developments he hitched his career to the rising fortune of one General Napoleon Bonaparte, who came to power as First Consul in November 1799. He then helped to bring about the Concordat of 1801 with the Vatican and in 1803 he was appointed to the lucrative position of Grand Chamberlain under Napoleon, by then Emperor, who in 1806 created him Prince of Benevento.

   Napoleon's decision to constantly ignore Talleyrand's cautious advice inevitably led to a split, and following the French invasion of Spain Talleyrand resigned, although he remained in the Imperial Council and continued as Grand Chamberlain until early 1809. When the Allies entered Paris in 1814, Talleyrand persuaded them to restore the Bourbons in the person of Louis XVIII, who duly made him Foreign Minister. He negotiated the first Treaty of Paris in May 1814, by which France, despite the defeat, was granted the French borders of 1792. He represented France at the Congress of Vienna between 1814–15, where he scored his greatest diplomatic triumphs. Winning the European powers to his principle of "legitimacy," namely, the restoration of Europe to its pre-revolutionary status, and shrewdly exploiting the dissension among the allies, he succeeded in taking part in the negotiations on equal terms with the principal victorious powers. Talleyrand remained in Vienna during the Hundred Days but resigned in September 1815, shortly after the second Bourbon Restoration, but in 1830, Louis Phillippe, whom he had helped to power, appointed Talleyrand to serve as Ambassador to London. He resigned in 1834, after having achieved the recognition of Belgium (1831) and signed the Quadruple Alliance of 1834.

   In many ways, Talleyrand remains the ultimate political survivor. His corruption was undeniable, but his pliability enabled him to hold power under the Ancien Régime, the Revolution, Napoleon, the Restoration and the July Monarchy. Depending on your point of view he can be seen as both the saviour of Europe in 1815 or damned as an opportunist and perhaps even a traitor. Nevertheless, Talleyrand's policy was aimed consistently – and often courageously – at the peace and stability of Europe as a whole.

10. When order was given for the High Seas Fleet to fight a last battle in the final days of the war, the sailors mutinied, refusing to become cannon fodder for the sake of what they saw as a meaningless gesture. On 28th October the mutineers took control of the city of Wilhelmshaven, forming an Arbeiter und Soldatenrat - a Workers' and Soldiers' Council, similar to the Russian Soviet. Workers and soldiers in other cities soon formed similar councils, which were dominated by Spartakist agitators. The leading Spartakist

agitators were Karl Liebknecht and Rosa Luxemburg. In Bavaria and Wuerttemberg, the Spartakists even took over state governments, transforming the respective kingdom in a Volksstaat (people's state).

The Spartakists believed that Germany was ripe for its own revolution, while the Social Democrats, who were trying to establish a stable German republic, were hard pushed to maintain order. After a series of strikes and street fighting, in January 1919 President Ebert decided to restore order by calling in the military, turning to squads of armed ex-soldiers (the Freikorps) to put down the Spartakist revolutionaries throughout Germany. The operation was carried out with brutal efficiency; Liebknecht and Luxemburg were both shot and killed, while Luxemburg's body was dumped in a canal.

11. Reuter's hopes that the Saar might remain a part of the Reich were to be short lived. Under the terms of the Treaty of Versailles, the Saar, a densely populated, Catholic, coal mining area of some 800,000 inhabitants was to be detached from Germany and placed under an international statute. Only in 1935 would the inhabitants of the Saar be afforded the opportunity to choose whether to return to the Reich, remain a *de facto* French protectorate under the auspices of the League of Nations, or become an integral part of France.

The main issue of the Saar plebiscite in January 1935 was whether the district would vote to join the Third Reich, a state that had abolished independent worker organisations and begun to violate its own Concordat of 1933 with the Vatican by infringing upon the rights of the Catholic Church. In spite of this the plebiscite was the greatest triumph for Adolf Hitler in a free election. The Nazis and their Catholic and right wing allies obtained 90.7 percent of the votes for the reincorporation of the Saar into Germany. Despite knowledge of what was going on under the Nazis in Germany, the overwhelming majority of voters, the bulk of whom were Catholic industrial workers and their family members, opted for reincorporation into the Reich.

12. Philipp Scheidemann began his career as a journalist before becoming a Reichstag delegate for the Social Democrats in 1903. It was not long before he rose to become one of the principle leaders of the party. During the First World War Scheidemann, along with Friedrich Ebert, was leader of the majority faction of the party, which continued to vote for war credits; at the same time he urged the negotiation of a compromise peace. When the Social Democrats were included in the cabinet for the first time in Prince Max of Baden's government in October 1918, Scheidemann entered the government as a minister without portfolio.

Following the Kaiser's abdication on 9th November, Prince Max resigned in favour of Ebert. Although the new government intended to support a constitutional monarchy, probably in the person of one of the Kaiser's grandsons, Scheidemann, concerned in the face of a possible Spartakist workers' revolution in Berlin, proclaimed the German Republic from a balcony in the Reichstag building that same day.

Scheidemann continued to serve as a leader in the Provisional Government, which followed for the next several months, and following the meeting of the National Assembly in Weimar in February 1919, Ebert was appointed President of Germany, and Scheidemann became Chancellor, in coalition with the German Democratic Party and the Catholic Centre Party. Scheidemann resigned in June along with the DDP due to disagreement with the Treaty of Versailles and never again served in the government, although he remained active in politics, serving as Mayor of Kassel from 1920-1925, and then again as a Reichstag delegate, where he exposed military opposition to the

Republic. Scheidemann went into exile following the Nazi takeover in 1933, dying in Denmark shortly after the outbreak of the Second World War.

13. In June 1919 Admiral Sir Sydney Robert Fremantle (1867-1958) commanded the British 1st Battle Squadron, which was then serving as the Guard Squadron at Scapa Flow. Fremantle entered the Royal Navy in 1881 and during World War One saw service from 1915-1918 in the Dardanelles, commanding the 9th Cruiser Squadron in 1916, the 2nd Cruiser Squadron in 1917 and the Aegean Squadron from 1917-1918. He was appointed Deputy Chief of Naval Staff from 1918-1919 and Vice Admiral commanding the 1st Battle Squadron from 1919-1921. He later served as Commander-in-Chief, Portsmouth Station from 1923-1926 and retired 1928. His autobiography, *My Naval Career: 1880 - 1928*, was published in 1949.

14. "The wife of the Commanding Officer wrote to me a few weeks before the sinking, as German officers' wives will, without much complaint: 'I have four children and am alone, you know what this means in these times, everything else I leave to you.' I went over to her husband in the *Markgraf* at once - he was angry at the letter. Of course, he would stay on in Scapa Flow, he wouldn't leave his ship. He kept his word. Honour him!" [Ludwig von Reuter]

15. Picquet (or Piquet) was established by the 16th century and was popular in France, Spain, and Italy, and spread to England under the name "Cent" (one hundred). It is a card game played by two persons with a deck of 32 cards - 7 (low) up to ace (high) in each suit. Each player receives twelve cards, and eight cards are left on the table face down. The non-dealer (the minor) discards from one to five cards and picks up an equal number from the table. The dealer (the major) is entitled to exchange the remaining number of cards. Trumps are not named. After the draw from the table, the hands are compared and points are given for point (the most cards in a suit), sequence (longest sequence), and highest set of three or four of a kind. Carte blanche, a hand without a face card, also scores points. Play of cards from the hands follows with points scored for tricks won. One hundred points wins. There are variations for three or four hands.

16. Donnington Hall is situated in Leicestershire, and during the First World War it served as a detention centre for high-ranking German officers.

17. In the mid-19th century Schleswig and Holstein were two German duchies that were under Danish rule. However Holstein's population was largely German-speaking and Schleswig's was a broad mix of Germans and Danes. In 1863 a war between Denmark and the German Confederation resulted in a victory for the Confederation and the acquisition of Schleswig and Holstein. Following the victory it was agreed that Austria would manage the duchy of Holstein and that Prussia would be in charge of the day to day running of Schleswig, but in 1866 further arguments about the administration of Schleswig-Holstein led to war breaking out between Austria and Prussia. This war lasted seven weeks and resulted in Prussian victory over the Austrians, which led to a clearer division between Austrian and German interests and forced the smaller states to align themselves alongside the Prussians. Following the Franco Prussian War of 1870-71 a wave of Germanic Nationalism swept through the German Confederation. After the victory over France in January of 1871, Prussia was able to persuade her partners within the German Confederation that unification was desirable and as a result Wilhelm of Prussia was proclaimed Emperor of Germany on January 18th 1871.

The Treaty of Versailles, however, radically altered the geography of Europe, much of it at the expense of Germany. Aside from the loss of all of her overseas colonies, Germany also lost 28,000 square miles of her European territory, along with some six million subjects, including parts of Schleswig, which were ceded to Denmark. Nordschleswig was eventually divided into two plebiscite zones, with 74.2 % of the northern voters opting to join Denmark, while 80% of the southern zone voters chose to remain a part of Germany. Nevertheless, 3,983 Sq.km of European territory was lost to Germany.

18. Lord Northcliffe (1865-1922) founded a print dynasty in 1888 as a freelance contributor to popular periodicals. His brother Harold (later 1st Viscount Rothermere) acted as the financial administrator of what became the world's largest periodical combine, the Amalgamated Press. Northcliffe bought the London *Evening News* in 1894, and went on to found the *Daily Mail* and *Daily Mirror* before seizing the *Times* in 1908. Northcliffe's interest in politics was fitful but intense. He campaigned vigorously against the Asquith Government and, like Lord Beaverbrook, for imperial preference (i.e. free trade within the British empire).

19. Baron Munchausen, whose full name was Hieronymous Karl Friedrich von Munchausen (1720-1797) served as a cavalry captain with a Russian regiment in two Turkish wars, and was known during his lifetime as an excellent raconteur of tales about war, hunting and travel adventures. From 1781 to 1783 a collection of such tales was published, with authorship generally attributed to the baron. An English version of the tales was published in 1785 under the title *Baron Munchausen's Narrative of His Marvellous Travels and Campaigns in Russia* but in 1824 it was revealed that the author of the English edition was one Rudolph Erich Raspe (1737-1794). Raspe had apparently become acquainted with the Baron at Gottingen, who, on retiring in 1760, lived on his estates at Bodenwerder and used to amuse himself and his friends, and puzzle the "quidnuncs" and the dull-witted, by relating extraordinary instances of his prowess as soldier and sportsman. Other authors used these stories as source material to exaggerate still further or to compose other tall tales of a similar mode and gradually Munchausen's name became associated with the amusingly preposterous story or the lie winningly told.

The baron also left his mark in medical circles. Munchausen syndrome, named after him, is defined as a condition characterised by the feigning of the symptoms of a disease or injury in order to undergo diagnostic tests, hospitalisation, or medical or surgical treatment.

20. HMS *Sandhurst* and HMS *Victorious* were the two British depot ships at Scapa Flow. HMS *Sandhurst* (7,654 tons) was originally the ex S.S. *Manipur*, a cargo ship built by Harland and Wolff in 1905 for T & J. Brocklebank, before being purchased by the Admiralty in 1915. HMS *Victorious* was an obsolete Majestic-class pre-dreadnought, built in 1893. By 1914 the 14,890-ton *Victorious*, which only mounted four twelve-inch guns, was of little or no military value and by 1916, after serving as a guard ship on the Humber and at Scapa Flow, was being utilised as a base and repair ship.

APPENDIX I

Report by the Leader of the Torpedo Boats on the Scuttling
By Korvettenkapitän Hermann Cordes

The Armistice expires at noon today, Saturday the 21st June 1919! Due to the confiscation of the wireless apparatus we are cut off from home and from the government. Any hour may bring a change, an important alteration of the situation, of which we will know nothing.

The English keep us in ignorance with malice aforethought. The German admiral is dependent on the English newspapers whose news is at least four days old.

The leading German statesmen, the President of the Reich and the Prime Minister, have all emphatically declared that the signing of the peace is impossible!

The English senior officer of the British squadron guarding us, Vice-Admiral Fremantle, must have been informed of the extension of the delay allowed for the signing of the treaty. Propriety and honourable dealing prescribed that the Germans should have been informed of this extension of the Armistice.

He did not do it! Whether this was on the advice of his government or not has not been decided.

We were kept in the dark!

Much to our astonishment the English squadron puts out to sea for exercises with accompanying destroyers, leaves the bay and turns over the duty of guarding us to two duty destroyers and the remaining drifters.

Harmlessness or knavery?

Union with other squadrons? Return in battle array and seizure by destroyers laid alongside under the cover of salvoes of heavy guns?

Or absence with the purpose of deluding us with certainty, to show us 'the hour is not critical, no sort of important development is to be expected?'

We cannot say, although by the statement of an English petty officer of the *Royal Sovereign* (as we were being taken prisoner) the intention was to take possession of the ships and torpedo boats, by force, on Monday the 23rd June!

Surmises and considerations of this sort were suddenly interrupted.

At eleven-twenty in the morning the signal 'Sink at once' comes from the *Emden*.

The die is cast!

The nearby groups are informed by light - proclaiming the order: 'Clear away for sinking ship,' and after a given time, in which the transmission and passing on of the message appears to be established, comes the prearranged executive signal:

'Carry on, "Z" - sink.'

As far as we can see from where we are, new war ensigns and unblemished commissioning pendants are hoisted close up in all the torpedo boats.

The word is also passed to the Sixth Flotilla, despite the difficulty of observation from them due to intervening land.

The keys of the Kingston valves and the inspection doors of the condensers fly overboard; the heavy inrush of water gurgles and roars, soon the floor plates in all holds are awash.

The boats are heeling! The opened scuttles incline nearer to the surface of the water. The water pours in eagerly!

Here a boat cants sharply up and then down. A second, with a noise of splitting and crashing, capsizes on to her neighbour. A third and fourth sink on an even keel!

In the part of Scapa Bay visible to us the ships are capsizing and sinking.

Friedrich der Grosse, which has much to atone for, is the first and is almost too quick!

'Belaying' the order - even had we wanted to - was now impossible.

The crews gather on the decks of the sinking ships, give three cheers for the German Fatherland and hoist out the boats, destined to bring them, in some cases, to their sacrificial death. They man the cutters peacefully and in an orderly manner, with the prescribed gear which they have had ready for days, in order to row to the land in accordance with their orders, where they would assemble and sit down to await the further sequence of events.

The published order, to conduct themselves towards the English guard boats or towards the military posts on shore with no sign of active or passive resistance, without any attempt to escape or movement, which might be construed as such, was everywhere followed to the letter.

Nevertheless, from all sides came at full speed: drifters, which had been lying in peace alongside *Sandhurst* and *Victorious*[20] and had cast off in a sort of hasty panic, armed fishing steamers, tugs, auxiliaries and the two guard destroyers *Vega* and *Vesper*, whose commanders, in a foaming rage, cast off from their buoys and, storming along among the unarmed German lifeboats, opened fire in defiance of all rights of international law and humanity, with their rifles, revolvers and machineguns.

The English seamen acted like madmen. Sailors, stokers, officers and civilians shouted and bellowed at one another.

There was no question of anyone being in charge. They shot wildly all around, aimed at one lifeboat, then left off the next minute in order to haul down and trample on the war ensign of a boat sinking in the vicinity, or indiscriminately to collect 'souvenirs' from the cabins and below decks, to steal and to pillage.

They hold a second and third rowing boat under deliberate rifle fire, recklessly direct they fire on the unarmed and helpless men jumping overboard and on those already in the water surrounded by the dead, and leave the wounded to their fate to make for another half-sunk torpedo boat in an attempt to cast off or cut its buoy adrift so as to get it into shallow water on the rocky shore.

Meanwhile the steam sirens of the drifters blare out in Morse code: 'German ships are sinking.'

The only thing that can be understood out of the shooting, the wild shouting and the furious gesticulations is the order: "Back to your ships at once - stop the sinking or you'll go to Hell!"

A few crews under the menace of weapons are compelled to return to their ships. Lifeboats and the life-saving, jackets they wore are taken away and the crews, on explaining that they have no means of preventing the sinking are held back on board the sinking boats by the rifles presented at them at the closest range and have "Then you shall die on board" shouted at them.

Captain MacLean, in the flotilla leader *Spenser*, rushes in from sea at full speed, no doubt as a result of some wireless signal reporting the situation, runs alongside *S132*, and orders the German commanding officer, Kapitänleutnant Oskar Wehr, to come to him aboard his ship; there he tells him that every German officer whose boat sinks will be shot on the spot, gives devilish-sounding, earnestly-meant, and unmistakable orders to his officers and has him and the remaining officers put in the bows of *S132* - opposite them is a detachment of Royal Marines with loaded rifles.

An English civilian presents a pistol at the head of Oberleutnant-zur-See Lampe, when the latter has got separated from his men and is just about to call out something to them, and pulls the trigger. The pistol goes off, the bullet grazes his temple.

V126's cutter, with Leutnant-zur-See Zaeschmar in charge, is fired at and hit by two English sailors who had climbed aboard *V45* and also by a drifter, which happens to be in the vicinity.

In spite of stopping at once, and in spite of shouts of surrender, the shooting continues.

In this way Torpedo Artificer Markgraf is killed by a shot in the head, and Chief Stoker Beike by one in the chest, while Chief Stoker Pankrath is so severely wounded that he dies the same day; three more petty officers are wounded, as are two stokers.

Oberleutnant-zur-See Karl Hoffmann, after returning, on board his boat under compulsion, has a pistol held to his chest; he is ordered to prevent his boat sinking; some of his men are forced down to the engine and ammunition spaces at the point of the pistol to take counter-measures or drown.

The three cutters of the group under Leutnant-zur-See Kluber are stopped by the English destroyer *F09*, which has all of her weapons, including her depth charges, manned, and cleared away. He is compelled to turn back by the revolver shots at short range fired by the English officers from their bridge.

The destroyer *F15*, hurrying to the scene, is also shooting and greets the jumping overboard of the crew of a cutter, which has just been hit by one of her salvoes, fired at a range of 150 metres with a bellow of cheering, and then directs her fire on a number of already wounded swimmers, who are crying loudly for help, at a range of 50 metres – a motor boat takes part in this shooting too.

A stoker is severely wounded by a shot in the stomach, Torpedo Artificer Peil by one in the leg, and other stokers are less badly wounded in the hands.

The English afford no sort of help to the wounded! They are meant to be drowned, to die like beasts.

The crews of the boats in the north exit from Gutter Sound now gather on the beach of the island of Fara, and those of the Third and Fourth Flotillas on board the *Sandhurst* and *Victorious* after the English have ceased their slaughter. Here they place themselves at the disposal of the English admiral in charge of the drifters and auxiliaries, a naval officer of the old school whose courteous and humane attitude is reported by Kapitänleutnant Steiner of the Third Flotilla.

As resistance was nowhere offered – we were unarmed, as any attempt at escape was recognised as useless and all orders, as far as they could in any way be followed, were carried out – the behaviour of the English cannot be described in any other way than as premeditated and bestial murder.

It is absurd to maintain that they were justified in using arms because we, who were the submissive ones, were supposed to have committed an act of war.

We began no fight. We did not break the Armistice. We disposed of our German property as seemed requisite to Admiral von Reuter in accordance with the political situation and in his position of supreme commander of a naval squadron, which should, by all appropriate rules of war, not be allowed to fall into the hands of the enemy.

Out of the torpedo boats there were:

Sunk at their buoys in deep water	32 boats
Sunk in shallow water, part of the boats above water	14 boats
Fate uncertain, but with important spaces flooded	2 boats
Salved, but damaged by water	2 boats

The casualties to be deplored are: 4 dead, 8 wounded, all of the Sixth Flotilla.

APPENDIX II

Remarks on Matters Spiritual at Scapa Flow
By Marine-Pfarrer (Naval Chaplain) Ronneberger

My tour of duty, lasting nearly five months, as chaplain to the interned squadron was under conditions as changeable as the weather in the Shetlands, between rain and sunshine.

It was a peculiar duty, rich in surprises and unusual features, but not without its uses to my office and person. Only he, who himself has for months at a time, day by day, oscillated so many paces forward and then the same number backwards on board his ship, who for months at a time has had no personal relationship with another ship, although the ships were within hail and lying impotently at their cables, can exactly understand what Scapa Flow meant to us internees. Always the same comfortless surroundings; cliffs, rocks, mountains, without ever a tree or shrub. The shore, so alluringly close and yet with no means of being reached. No freedom of movement, always the same people with the same sorrows and cares and among them so very many men, psychologically sick, who, in the November days of the revolution, had counted on fraternisation with the English. And now what a disillusionment! Nothing of international unity! Taken prisoner and scorned! And what's more even after the example given by the Soldiers' Council organisation at home, which sowed anxiety and dissension when above all things a conscious unity in attitude should have been the case. In this atmosphere I came as a sort of compensatory impetus. I was not received with joy, but rather in a spirit of mistrust. How could it, however, be otherwise when, even before my arrival, the Head Soldiers' Council of the interned fleet caused a circular letter to be sent to all ships, in which they pointed out the danger of the presence of a chaplain and in which they agitated against me personally. And why? Because I had directed the publication, during the war, of the war newspaper *On Outpost Duty* in the national interest. 'Naval Chaplain Ronneberger was the editor of the paper *On Outpost Duty*,' is how it stands in the circular letter sent to the ships' companies. The man is not to be trusted politically. So have a care! And these are the lines on which the Head Soldiers' Council decided my work was to be carried out:

> "His activities extend only to purely Church and instructional subjects. Politics are forbidden him by us. The Soldiers' Council exercises the sharpest control in this connection and is authorised to refuse him permission to speak in case of non-compliance with their injunction, or (prudently a loophole was left here) other counter-measures will be taken. Attendance at church services and at lectures, etc., to be voluntary."

That was the greeting I received as I entered on my office. My arrival was announced to the ships in the daily routine orders, and they were told to communicate with me direct as regards requests for church services. But in the

120

first fourteen days I was left undisturbed. No ship expressed a wish for any sort of church service. But, after their mistrust had been overcome, the desire for more services made itself felt, at first gradually, but increasing as time went by, so that for the Easter festival twenty services were announced and confirmed officially in the daily routine orders. Out of twenty-six battleships and cruisers, twenty-two had divine service. Four ships gave up all claim to my offices. In all, in four months fifty-two services, twenty-five lectures and thirty instructional classes were held. The attendance at divine service was always voluntary and amounted to 75 per cent on an average in certain ships, especially in the torpedo boats, where it rose to 95 per cent. As regards the form they took, it was found necessary to adapt them to circumstances. It was found very disagreeable having to dispense with any musical accompaniment; for this reason, where men's choirs could not be organised, concertinas, accordions or violins have to supply the accompaniment. A part of the services, which came to be usual, was a sort of talk in which professional and family affairs, and questions of provision for the future, were discussed.

Apart from the above only burials came into my province, in regard to which I had to interview the English naval commander three times. In two cases, which occurred before my arrival, the English naval chaplain had officiated at the burial. After my arrival I was charged with this duty and had permission to go ashore for this purpose. In this way our comrades were laid in their last sleep according to the German custom, although in foreign soil in the naval cemetery of Lyness on Hoy. No German was permitted to take a part, neither officer nor man, except for me, personally. Another of those endearing characteristics that the English at that time displayed to us! I rendered the honours to the departed quite alone. As my last visit to the cemetery showed me that the German graves were left quite uncared for, I suggested to the men that a worthy monument was needed to embellish the graves. A collection, which was carried out on board all the ships, produced the gift of 1,500 Marks, with which I bought a memorial stone on my return to the homeland. It was, however, sunk with the fleet, as it had not then been landed.

Finally it may be of interest to note the Soldiers' Councils, stimulated by the Soldiers' Council on board the light cruiser *Emden*, occupied themselves with the question of the retention of chaplains in the navy. For those days, since the revolution, when anything to do with divine worship had, so to speak, been degraded by routine orders, when it was considered good form to be thought a free-thinker, it was a noticeable step forward that the men, directed by their comrades, ordered a collection in order to have a part in the funeral. In a circular letter issued by the Soldiers' Council of the *Emden* 'to all' on the 26th April it stood as follows:

"It must be appreciated that it is possible that the Church will be disestablished in Republican Germany and thus we shall eventually be deprived of our chaplains in the fleet. The attendance at divine service is voluntary and should also remain voluntary in the State navy for all time. Here especially, at

Scapa Flow, many members of the crews have taken the opportunity of attending voluntarily from time to time at divine service. In order that we may be certain of having a fleet and squadron chaplain in the new state navy, who will not be privately but publicly appointed by the government, as was the case in former days, we would like to approach the squadron commander and the Head Soldiers' Council, after confirmation by individual ships and torpedo boats, with the request that immediate steps be taken in conjunction with the Admiralty and the government so that chaplains may be provided for in the establishment of the navy, not only for ships at home but also for those abroad. The chaplain should not only be responsible for holding services but should also give lectures of a non-political kind. An example of how necessary a chaplain is, is provided by the funerals of three of our comrades who were buried ashore here. Chaplain Ronneberger was present and officiated. They were buried as true German soldiers with military honours.'

APPENDIX III
Times at which the ships were sunk on the 21st June 1919

A:	Sunk:	Time of Sinking
	Battlecruisers:	
	Derfflinger	2.45 pm
	Hindenburg	5.00 pm
	Moltke	1.10 pm
	Seydlitz	1.50 pm
	Von der Tann	2.15 pm
	Battleships:	
	Bayern	2.30 pm
	Friedrich der Grosse	12.16 pm
	Grosser Kurfürst	1.30 pm
	Kaiser	1.25 pm
	Kaiserin	2.00 pm
	König	2.00 pm
	König Albert	12.54 pm
	Kronprinz Wilhelm	1.15 pm
	Markgraf	4.45 pm
	Prinzregent Luitpold	1.30 pm
	Light Cruisers:	
	Bremse	2.30 pm
	Brummer	1.05 pm
	Cöln	1.50 pm
	Dresden	1.30 pm
	Karlsruhe	3.50 pm

B: Not Sunk:

Battleship *Baden*:	Towed to land in a sinking condition
Light Cruiser *Emden*:	Towed to land in a sinking condition
Light Cruiser *Frankfurt*:	Towed to land in a sinking condition
Light Cruiser *Nürnberg*:	Cable slipped and driven ashore still floating

Torpedo Boats
A: Sunk at their buoys
    32 Torpedo Boats
B: In shallow water, and partly above water
    14 Torpedo Boats
C: Fate uncertain but important compartments flooded
    (*S60, V80*)
    2 Torpedo Boats
D: Beached, but apparently damaged under water
    (*S132, G102*) 2 Torpedo Boats

APPENDIX IV
List of the Interned Ships and Torpedo Boats and their Commanders and Leaders

Editor's Note: In order to retain as great a feel for the original text as possible, each officer's rank throughout the book has been kept to the original German. As a guide, the nearest British equivalent of the German ranks is as follows:

Vizeadmiral - Vice-Admiral
Konteradmiral - Rear-Admiral
Kommodore - Commodore
Kapitän-zur-See - Captain
Fregattenkapitän - Commander
Korvettenkapitän - Lieutenant Commander
Kapitänleutnant - Lieutenant
Oberleutnant-zur-See - Sub-Lieutenant

Staff on board *Emden*

Officer commanding the Interned Squadron	Konteradmiral von Reuter
Chief of Staff	Fregattenkapitän Oldekop
Admiral's Staff Officer	Kapitänleutnant Lautenschlager
Flag-Lieutenant	Oberleutnant-zur-See Schilling
Squadron Paymaster	Stabszahlmeister Habicht
Naval Advocate	Marine-Kriegsgerichtsrat Loesch (Leutnant, Militia)

On board *Markgraf*

Squadron Engineer	Marine Oberstabs-Ing. Faustmann

On board *Prinzregent Luitpold*

Squadron Surgeon	Marine-Stabsarzt Dr. Lange

Flagship Emden

Commanding Officer	Kapitänleutnant Ehlers

Battleships	**Commanding Officers**
Baden	Korvettenkapitän Zirzow
Bayern	Kapitänleutnant Meißner
Friedrich der Grosse	Korvettenkapitän von Wachter
Grosser Kurfürst	Kapitänleutnant Beer
Kaiser	Kapitänleutnant Wippern
Kaiserin	Korvettenkapitän Viertel
König	Korvettenkapitän Junkermann
König Albert	Korvettenkapitän Böhmer
Kronprinz Wilhelm	Kapitänleutnant Becker
Markgraf	Korvettenkapitän Schumann
Prinzregent Luitpold	Kapitänleutnant von Reiche

124

Battlecruisers	Commanding Officers
Derfflinger	Korvettenkapitän Pastuszyk
Hindenburg	Korvettenkapitän Heyden
Moltke	Kapitänleutnant Erelinger
Seydlitz	Kapitänleutnant Brauer
Von der Tann	Kapitänleutnant Wollanke

Light Cruisers	Commanding Officers
Bremse	Oberleutnant-zur-See Schacke
Brummer	Kapitänleutnant Prahl
Cöln	Kapitänleutnant Heinemann
Dresden	Kapitänleutnant Fabricius
Frankfurt	Kapitänleutnant Beesel
Karlsruhe	Kapitänleutnant Ruville
Nürnberg	Kapitänleutnant Georgii

Torpedo Boats

Leader of the Torpedo Boats — Korvettenkapitän Hermann Cordes aboard *S138*

Flag-Lieutenant — Kapitänleutnant Schniewind aboard *S138*
Squadron Engineer — Marine-Oberstabs Ing. Halwe aboard *H145*
Squadron Paymaster — Marine-Zahlm. d. Res. Horn aboard *S138*

First Torpedo Boat Flotilla

Leader — Kapitänleutnant Henrici aboard *G40*

G38, G39, G40, G86, S32, V129.

Second Torpedo Boat Flotilla

Leader — Kapitänleutnant Menche aboard *B110*

B109, B110, B111, B112, G101, G102, G103, V100.

Third Torpedo Boat Flotilla

Leader — Kapitänleutnant Steiner aboard *S54*

S53, S54, S55, S91, V70, V73, V81, V82.

Sixth Torpedo Boat Flotilla

Leader — Kapitänleutnant Wehr aboard *V44*

Half-leader (Eleventh Half-Flotilla) — Kapitänleutnant von Bonin aboard *S131*

S49, S50, S131, S132, V43, V44, V45, V46, V125, V126, V127, V128.

125

Seventh Torpedo Boat Flotilla

Leader	Korvettenkapitän Hermann Cordes aboard *S138*.
Half-leader (Thirteenth Half-Flotilla)	Kapitänleutnant Roslik aboard *S56*.
Half-leader (Fourteenth Half-Flotilla)	Kapitänleutnant Reimer aboard *S136*

G89, G92, H145, S56, S65, S136, S137, S138, V78, V83.

Seventeenth Torpedo Boat Flotilla

Half-leader	Kapitänleutnant Ganguin aboard *V80*

S36, S51, S52, S60, V80.

BIBLIOGRAPHY

Bowman, Gerald. *The Man Who Bought a Navy*. George G. Harrap & Co., 1964.

Brown, Malcolm. & Meehan, Patricia. *Scapa Flow: The Reminiscences of Men and Women Who Served in the Two World Wars*. Allen Lane The Penguin Press, 1968.

Fremantle, Admiral Sir Sydney: *My Naval Career*. Hutchinson, 1949.

George, S. C. *Jutland to Junkyard*. Patrick Stephen Ltd., 1973.

Gröner, Erich. *German Warships 1815–1945*.

(Volume One: Major Surface Vessels). Conway, 1990.

Hewison, William S. *This Great Harbour: Scapa Flow*. The Orkney Press, 1985.

Hoehling, A. A. *The Great War at Sea: The Dramatic Story of Naval Warfare 1914 - 1918*. Arthur Barker Ltd, 1965.

Janes Fighting Ships (1919)

Macdonald, Rod. *Dive Scapa Flow*, Mainstream Publishing, 1995.

Miller, James. *Scapa*. Birlinn Ltd., 2000.

Ruge, Vice-Admiral Friedrich. *Scapa Flow 1919: The End of the German Fleet*. Ian Allan, 1973.

Smith, Peter L. *The Naval Wrecks of Scapa Flow*. The Orkney Press, 1989.

van der Vat, Dan. *The Grand Scuttle: The Sinking of the German Fleet at Scapa Flow in 1919*. Waterfront, 1986.

ADDITIONAL SOURCES

Orkney Library Photographic Archive, Kirkwall
The National Archives, Kew
Naval Historical Branch, H.M. Naval Base, Portsmouth
The *Orcadian/Orkney Herald*

The publishers would especially like to thank the von Reuter family for granting access to their private papers, Dan van der Vat for his additional advice and David Mackie at the Orkney Library Photographic Archive for generously placing the library's photographic collection at their disposal.

INDEX

Adalbert (Prince) 9, 10
Admiralty (British) 41, 43, 47, 55,
    63, 69, 72, 84, 87, 88, 92,
    100
Admiralty (German) 9, 33, 66, 69,
    72, 74, 89, 92, 94, 121
Allies 16, 17, 19, 26, 29, 74, 96
Alloa Shipbreaking Company 105,
    108
Amazone, SMS 9
Arminius, SMS 9
Armistice 16, 19, 20, 21, 26, 27,
    28, 29, 35, 40, 42, 43, 48,
    56, 68, 78, 84, 85, 90, 91,
    92, 95, 96, 116
Armistice Commission 31, 34, 48,
    50
Atomic Bomb 109
Aufklärungsgruppe (1st) 15
Aufklärungsgruppe (2nd) 14, 15
Aufklärungsgruppe (4th) 13, 14
Austria 9
Baden, SMS 21, 30, 50, 81, 83,
    86, 100
Baltic 27, 70
Battle Squadron, 1st (British) 20
Bavaria 9
Bayern, SMS 37, 81, 86, 108
Beatty, Sir David (Admiral) 13,
    17, 30, 31, 32, 35, 42, 47
Beck Brothers 89
Beike (Chief Stoker) 118
Belgium 85
Ben Urie 100
Berlin 12, 50, 89, 92
Berlin, SMS 13
Bismarck, Otto von 9
Blücher, SMS 13
Bornstedt Graveyard 23
Bremen, S.S. 48
Bremen 89
Bremse, SMS 81, 106
Brockelmann, Johanna 12
Brummer, SMS 80, 109
Cava 39, 103, 108
Clemenceau
    (French Prime Minister) 91
Clyde (River) 109
Coburg 9, 89
Cöln, SMS 34, 36, 109
Compiègne 16
Cordes, Hermann
    (Korvettenkapitän) 32, 65,
    91, 116
Cox, Ernest 100, 101, 102, 103,
    104, 105, 106, 107, 108
Cromarty Firth 84
Denmark 9, 23, 27
Depression, The 108
Derfflinger, SMS 12, 13, 16, 34,
    81, 108, 109
Dogger Bank, Battle of 13
Dominik, (Kommodore) 18, 49

Donnington Hall
    (prisoner-of-war camp) 21,
    88, 89, 92, 94, 97
Dreadnought, HMS 12
Dresden, SMS 30, 108
Dresky (Rittmeister von) 87
Duren 89
East Prussia 23
Elze (Kapitänleutnant) 53, 61
Emden, SMS 19, 21, 53, 57, 61,
    63, 73, 76, 79, 80, 81, 86,
    100, 116, 121
Emperor of India, HMS 38
English Government 35, 41, 43,
    47, 69, 74, 84, 90, 93, 94,
    95, 96, 97
Entente 26, 27, 28, 34, 43, 45,
    50, 63, 68, 70, 74, 78, 79,
    87, 90, 92, 93, 95, 96, 97
Erin, HMS 100
Esterkand (Catholic Chaplain) 65
F09 (British Destroyer) 118
F15 (British Destroyer) 118
Faustmann
    (Engineer Commander) 65
Firth of Forth 13, 17, 26, 27, 28,
    29, 30, 31, 32, 33, 34, 36,
    37, 38, 47
Fleet Laws 10
Fourth Flotilla 119
Fourth Squadron 34, 38
France 9, 10, 12, 23
Franco-Prussian War 9, 10
Frankfurt, SMS 21, 81, 100
Frauenlob, SMS 13, 14
Frederick the Great 28
Frederick William IV (King) 9
Friedrich Carl, SMS 9
Friedrich der Grosse, SMS 16, 17,
    18, 19, 32, 34, 38, 57, 60,
    61, 79, 80, 108, 117
Fremantle, Sir Sydney Robert
    (Vice Admiral) 20, 21, 82,
    88, 90, 91, 116
G104 101
General Strike 105
German Army 10
German Government 19, 27, 43,
    50, 57, 68, 69, 70, 71, 72,
    74, 77, 78, 88, 90, 91, 92,
    93, 94, 96, 97
German Republic 16, 121
Germany 9, 10, 12, 15, 18, 19,
    20, 21, 22, 40, 77, 87
Giessler (Defence Minister) 22
Gillmann (Kapitän) 94
Goethe, 23, 77
Goette, (Vice Admiral) 49
Graf Waldersee, S.S. 48
Grand Fleet 12, 14, 15, 17, 31,
    35-36,
Great Britain 10, 12, 23
Greek King 11
Grosser Kurfürst, SMS 81, 108

Gulf Stream 39
Guben, 9
Gusow 89
Gutter Sound 119
Habicht (Paymaster) 65
Hannover, SMS 14
Head Soldier's Councillor 33, 41,
    46, 50, 51, 53, 55, 57-58, 60
Heinrich (Kommodore) 63
Helgoland/Heligoland 17, 26, 28,
    34
Hermann Künne (Z19) 23
Hessen, SMS 14
High Seas Fleet 12, 14, 15, 16,
    17, 18, 19, 23, 26, 27, 28,
    29, 32, 43, 47, 100, 108, 109
Hindenburg, SMS 34, 81, 100,
    101, 102, 103, 104, 105,
    106, 107
Hipper, Franz von (Admiral) 12,
    13, 15, 16, 17, 29, 30, 31
Hodges, Michael (Commodore)
    36
Hoffmann, Karl
    (Oberleutnant-zur-See) 118
Holland 16, 23, 27
Hoy 121
Hubertusburg Castle 28
Hull 22, 97, 98
Imperial Navy Office 12
Indomitable, HMS 13
Jade (River) 98
Jutland, Battle of (Skaggerak) 11,
    13, 14, 15
Kageneck (Graf) 89
Kaiser, SMS 105, 106
Kaiserin, SMS 86, 108
Karlsruhe, SMS 109
Kiel 15, 16, 17
Kluber (Leutnant-zur-See) 118
König, SMS 16, 30, 109
König Albert, SMS 80, 108
König Wilhelm, SMS 9
Königsberg 23
Königsberg, SMS 14, 15, 29
Kriegsmarine 23, 108
Kronprinz SMS 9
Kronprinz Wilhelm, SMS 109
Lampe (Oberleutnant-zur-See)
    118
Lange (Staff Surgeon) 65
Liebknecht, Karl 50
Lion, HMS 13
Lisboa, SS 22
Lloyd George, David (British
    Prime Minister) 93, 94, 97
Lobsien 89, 91, 92
Loesch (Naval Magistrate) 65
Loreley, SMS 11
Lorraine 9
Luxemburg, Rosa 50
Lyness 101, 105, 106, 108, 121
Mackensen, SMS 30
MacLean, Colin (Captain) 118

Madden, Charles (Admiral) 36,
47
Markgraf, SMS 16, 65, 81, 83,
86, 109
Markgraf (Torpedo Artificer) 118
Marwitz, von der 28
May Island 17, 30, 31
Metal Industries 108, 109
Meurer, Hugo (Konteradmiral) 29,
30-31
Minister of Defence (German) 58,
59
Moltke, SMS 12, 34, 80, 100,
103, 104, 105, 106
Monts, Alexander von 10
Munchausen, Baron 94
München, SMS 13, 14
Narvik 23
Nau (Major) 87
New Zealand, HMS 13
Nigg (prisoner-of-war camp) 21,
86
Northcliffe Group 92
Northern Lights 67
North Sea 10, 12, 13, 17, 26, 27,
28, 30, 33, 34, 98
Norway 23, 27
Nürnberg, SMS 21, 81, 86, 100
Oberkommando 10
Oder (river) 9
Oldekop, Ivan (Fregattenkapitän)
32, 79, 91
On Outpost Duty 120
Orion, HMS 100
Orkney Islands 18, 39, 67, 101,
109
Ostfriesland, SMS 15
Oswestry (prisoner-of-war camp)
21, 87, 88, 92
Pankrath (Chief Stoker) 118
Paris Peace Conference 19, 63,
71
Peace Treaty 74, 78, 90, 92, 93,
94, 97
Peil (Torpedo Artificer) 119
Pentland Skerries 38
Perth 66
Piraeus 11
Poland 23
Potsdam 22, 23
Press (English) 71, 73, 77, 78,
79, 84, 87, 90, 91, 92, 95,
946, 97, 116
Press (French) 93, 94
Press (German) 29, 90, 93, 94,
96, 97
Princess Royal, HMS 13
Pinzregent Luitpold, SMS 107,
108
Prinz Adalbert, SMS 9
Prussia 9, 10
Queen Elizabeth, HMS 12, 29
Raeder, Erich 11, 23
Red Guard 50, 56, 57
Regensburg, SMS 16
Reich Naval Office 18, 48, 49, 50,
51, 54, 55, 57, 65

Reichsmarine 22
Reichsmarineamt 10
Reichstag 10, 11, 74, 90, 94, 95
Reparations Protocol 22
Reuter, Alexander von 10
Reuter, Derfflinger von 22, 23
Reuter, Eduard von 9
Reuter, Ernst von 10
Reuter, Helene von 9
Reuter, Johanna von
(née Brockelmann)
Reuter, Ludwig von 9-23, 77, 85,
100, 108, 109, 119
Reuter, Wolfgang von 22, 23
Reuter, Yorck von 22, 23
Revenge, HMS 20, 21, 82, 85, 90,
96
Robetson, J.W. 100
Rogge (Staff Engineer) 86
Room 40 (Admiralty) 13
Ronneberger, (Protestant
Chaplain) 65, 120, 122
Rostock, SMS 14
Rosyth 101, 105, 108
Royal Marines 83, 118
Royal Oak, HMS 84
Royal Sovereign, HMS 116
Ruffhold 89
Russia 10, 12, 23
Russo-Japanese War 35
Rustringen 98
S132 118
Saar District 70
Salvage Unit 3 101
Sandhurst, HMS 117, 119
Sans Souci 23
Saxony 22
Scapa Flow 12, 17, 18, 21, 23,
26, 29, 30, 38, 39, 40, 43,
44, 45, 46, 47, 48, 49, 50,
51, 55, 66, 67, 72, 74, 79,
83, 84, 88, 89, 92, 94, 95,
96, 98, 100, 107, 108, 109,
117, 119, 121
Scapa Flow: das Grab der
deutschen Flotte 22
Scapa Flow Salvage and
Shipbreaking Company 100
Scarborough 12
Schacke, Oberleutnant–zur-See
81
Scheer, Reinhardt (Admiral) 15
Scheidemann, Philipp (German
Chancellor) 16, 20, 74, 95
Schiller, Friedrich 20, 23
Schillig Roads 15, 17, 27, 31, 32
Schilling (Oberleutnant-zur-See)
83, 94
Schleswig-Holstein 89
Schloss Gauernitz 22
Schumann (Korvettenkapitän) 83,
86
Seven Years' War 28
Seydlitz, SMS 12, 13, 34, 81, 83,
100, 105, 106
Sheppy, Isle of 100
Shetland County Council 100

Sierra Ventana, S.S. 48
Sixth Flotilla 81, 117, 119
Skaggerak, Battle of (Jutland) 13,
34, 37, 73, 98
Soldiers' and Workers' Council
37
Southampton, HMS 14
South Dogger Light Ship 30
Spain 26
Spanish Government 26
Spartakists 50, 56
Spenser, HMS 117
Spichern Heights, 9
Stettin, SMS 13, 14
Stromness 100
Steiner (Kapitänleutnant) 119
Stuttgart, SMS 13
Swiss Embassy 88, 91
Sweden 9, 27
Talleyrand 44
Tannenberg, Battle of 23
Tauroggen, Treaty of 28
Third Flotilla 119
Third Reich 23
Third Squadron 34
Thüringen, SMS 15
Tiger, HMS 13
Times, The 19, 77, 78, 85, 90
Tirpitz, Alfred von (Admiral) 10
Trotha, Adolph von
(Konteradmiral) 97
Turkish Sultan 11
U-boats 14, 15, 16, 71, 87
United States 16, 26
V30 34
V45 118
V70 101
Vega, HMS 117
Vesper, HMS 117
Victorious, HMS 117, 119
Von der Tann, SMS 16, 34, 81,
107, 108
Wallenstein, Death of 20
War Office 93
Watch Command (WAKO) 48
Wehr, Oskar (Kapitänleutnant)
118
Weimar 89
Wernig (Kapitänleutnant) 94
Weserübung (Operation) 23
Wilhelm II (Kaiser) 10, 15, 16, 19,
23, 68, 84, 100, 108
Wilhelmshaven 9, 15, 16, 17, 18,
22, 26, 27, 31, 33, 40, 42,
51, 56, 59, 60, 66, 97, 98
Wilhelmshaven Naval Dockyard
12
Workers' and Soldiers' Councils
16, 17, 18, 27, 33, 41, 43,
44, 46, 51, 53, 54, 56, 57,
58, 59, 60, 61, 62, 119, 121,
122
World War II 11, 23, 109
Yorck, General 28
Yorck, SMS 12
Zaeschmar (Leutnant-zur-See)
118